Global Labour and Employment Relations

Experiences and Challenges

Edited by Dong-One Kim and Mia Rönnmar

ILERA
International Labour
and Employment
Relations Association

PARKYOUNG
publishing&company

GLOBAL LABOUR AND EMPLOYMENT RELATIONS
Experiences and Challenges

Parkyoung Publishing Company
36, Saemunan-ro 3-gil, Jongno-gu, Seoul, 03173, Korea
Tel 82-2-733-6771
Fax 82-2-736-4818

First Published in 2020
Printed in Seoul, Korea
ISBN-13: 979-11-303-0879-1

For subscriptions to this book, please contact the sole distributor,
PARKYOUNG Publishing & Company.
E-mail: pys@pybook.co.kr

CONTENTS

CONTRIBUTORS

Janice Bellace, Professor Emeritus, University of Pennsylvania, USA, ILERA President 2009-2012.

Friedrich Furstenberg, Professor Emeritus, Bonn University, Germany, ILERA President 1983-1986.

Tadashi Hanami, Professor Emeritus, Sophia University, Japan, ILERA President 1998-2000.

Evance Kalula, Professor Emeritus, University of Cape Town, South Africa, ILERA President 2012-2015.

Dong-One Kim, Professor, Korea University, Korea, ILERA President 2015-2018.

Thomas A. Kochan, Professor, Massachusetts Institute of Technology, USA, ILERA President 1992-1995.

Russell Lansbury, Professor Emeritus, University of Sydney, Australia, ILERA President 2006-2009.

John Niland, President Emeritus, University of New South Wales, Australia, ILERA President 1989-1992.

Mia Rönnmar, Professor, Lund University, Sweden, ILERA President 2018-2021.

Tiziano Treu, Professor Emeritus, Catholic University of Milan, Italy, ILERA President 1995-1998.

Manfred Weiss, Professor Emeritus, Goethe University, Germany, ILERA President 2000-2003.

Preface

Harry Katz

This is a provocative collection of chapters by a number of the former presidents of the International Labour and Employment Relations Association (ILERA). The essays discuss how the field of industrial relations is evolving and the implications for ILERA. The contributors are all leading scholars so their views carry deserved weight beyond that due from their ILERA administrative service.

It is striking how similar are the views of the former presidents even though they reside in a wide range of countries and their academic sub-fields differ across labour relations, economics, and the law. All the chapters note similar far-reaching changes in the nature of work, many induced by alterations in technology, such as the rise of computer-mediated "platform" work, and pressures from globalization, leading to an increasing importance of labour rights and global supply chains.

The former ILERA presidents urge academics to adjust their research to focus more extensively on those trends while maintaining allegiance to the perspective and values that originally motivated the field of industrial relations. To do that research will necessarily be multidisciplinary and make use of a variety of methodologies. The former presidents recognize that the coverage of collective bargaining and union representation has declined substantially, and continues to decline in nearly all countries. Nonetheless, the field of industrial relations continues to provide important insights into the changing nature of work including how those changers affect workers and the workers' responses. The continuing relevance of industrial relation springs from the fact that conflict at the workplace and higher levels has not abetted and in fact, there are signs of the spread of new forms of collective representation including affinity groups and wildcat protests.

There is a common trend toward income inequality across developed and developing economies. And while there is room for debate regarding the degree to which union decline has contributed to that inequality, there is wide recognition of contention at workplace and broader social levels regarding the distribution of economic progress and the extent of employee voice in economic decisions. On these issues and so many others, the former ILERA presidents demonstrate that industrial relations has much to say.

Introduction

Mia Rönnmar

01

Aim and Context of the Book

This book contains a unique collection of chapters written by ten past-presidents of the International Labour and Employment Relations Association (ILERA). The initiator of the book is Professor Dong-One Kim, immediate past-president of ILERA. The celebration of the 50th anniversary of ILERA forms an important background to the book. Furthermore, the past-presidents presented and discussed their chapters during a special Anniversary Plenary Session at the 18th ILERA World Congress, hosted by Kim and held in Seoul in July 2018. The main theme of the World Congress was "Employment for a Sustainable Society: What is to be Done?"

The past-presidents, from different parts of the world, are all distinguished and leading researchers and experts in our field. Their work has not only contributed greatly to and inspired new scholarship, but it has also had important implications for policy and practice in the areas of employment relations, labour law and human resource management at national, regional and international levels.

In their chapters, the past-presidents reflect on the past, present and future of ILERA and the field of labour and employment relations, and highlight both potentials and challenges.

ILERA was founded in 1966 as the International Industrial Relations Association (IIRA). According to its Articles of Organization, its general purpose is to promote the study of labour and employment relations throughout the world, by such means as encouraging the establishment of national associations; facilitating the publication and spread of information about significant developments in research and education; and, organizing international and regional congresses.[1] In 2009, the first female ILERA President, Professor Janice Bellace, took office, serving as an important pioneer and role model. After a long and inclusive process of dialogue, the association changed its name to ILERA in 2010. The name change reflects a recognition of the broadening of the scope of the association and the field of research to fully include, for example, developing countries; labour and all those who work (in paid employment, self-employment, informal work or the care economy etc.); and a multitude of different topical issues, such as the transnational movement of labour; non-standard work; labour market regulation; trade and labour standards; and discrimination in employment.[2]

From the very beginning, ILERA has collaborated closely and fruitfully with the International Labour Organization (ILO). The International Institute of Labour Studies was one of the founding institutions of ILERA. An ILO-official serves as the Secretary-General of ILERA, and the ILERA Secretariat is based at the ILO in Geneva and provides invaluable support to the association. In 2018, at the 18th World Congress in Seoul a new Memorandum of Understanding (MoU) between ILERA and the ILO was signed and celebrated. The MoU aims at enhancing collaboration between the parties in different ways.

The second section provides, by reasons of space, only a brief presentation of the authors and the content of their chapters, in the chronological order of their presidency. The third section presents some common themes and reflections on the future outlook.

The Chapters

Friedrich Furstenberg from Germany was President between 1983 and 1986. In his chapter, "My Experience with the IIRA (ILERA)," he discusses the traditional and future focus of ILERA and labour and employment relations, and highlights, for example, the importance of paying attention to changes in the labour force; labour market structures and processes; employment policies; interest representation in the labour market; contents and structure of negotiations; and, the key role played by the notion of decent work. Furstenberg also presents his important initiative to establish "Study Groups." The Study Groups - active also in between world and regional congresses - have developed into global networks of labour and employment relations scholars, resulting in numerous research projects and publications.

John Niland from Australia was President between 1989 and 1992. In his chapter, "Times of Change and Deep Transformation: IIRA 9th World Congress, Sydney 1992," he revisits the themes, papers and experiences from the World Congress in Sydney, and reflects on past and current trends of change and deep transformation, both in relation to our field of research and in relation to the realities of the world of work and labour and employment relations. He illustrates how the fate of trade unionism; the future of industrial relations as a field of study; and, the threat - or opportunity - posed by the rise of human resource management were key trends discussed at the World Congress. These trends are also discussed in relation to the development of Australian labour and employment relations.

Thomas A. Kochan from the US was president between 1992 and 1995. In his chapter, "Challenges and Opportunities Facing ILERA and our Field," he reflects on the legacy of ILERA and explores ways to advance the field of labour and employment relations in the years ahead. He addresses a number of key aspects, such as the composition and notion of the workforce and the worker; the trend from labour market dualism to fissurization of employment; the future of work and technological development; globalization; worker voice, social dialogue and bargaining power; rethinking management roles and norms; and a move toward a new social contract. One conclusion is that ILERA and labour and employment relations scholars have a lot to offer - and a lot to do - if we are to improve the world of work for generations to come.

Tiziano Treu from Italy was President between 1995 and 1998. In his chapter, "Employment for a Sustainable Society: What is to be Done?," he uses the EU and European developments and experiences as an example to discuss the speed of change and the depth of the challenges that labour law and employment relations, and our field of study, are facing today. He emphasizes the need for comparative research, and explores issues, such as the European policy of flexicurity; the impact of the digital revolution on the future of work; new risks for health and safety and for personal privacy; the impact of change on labour unions and collective agreements; decentralization of collective bargaining; and global trade and fundamental rights.

Tadashi Hanami from Japan was President between 1998-2000. In his chapter, "The West and the East in Industrial Relations and Labour Law," he discusses the importance of globalization and trends of convergence and divergence. He argues for the need to include perspectives from all parts of the world (East and West; North and South; and Developed and Developing) in the work of ILERA and the field of labour and employment relations. He also points to current trends toward populism and post-orientalism.

Manfred Weiss from Germany was President between 2000-2003. In his chapter, "Challenges for Labour Law and Industrial Relations," his focus is on two key challenges to labour law and industrial relations today, namely, the deficiencies of international labour regulation and the digitalization of work. His aim is not to present possible solutions, but rather to identify challenges and the future activities of ILERA. Weiss discusses the problem of enforcing international labour standards and the role of private actors and global supply chains in this context. Furthermore, he highlights different forms of digital work and the need to address a number of issues, such as the scope of labour law; training; working time and health and safety and working; privacy and collective representation.

Russell Lansbury from Australia was President between 2006-2009. In his chapter, "The International Labour and Employment Relations Association (ILERA) at Fifty: the Journey So Far and the Way Ahead," he provides a historical account and analysis of the evolution of ILERA through its phases of formative development, consolidation and maturation and reorientation and revitalization. He argues for the need to maintain a multidisciplinary approach to issues of work and the employment relationship and to connect the micro-level issues at the workplace level with macro-level issues in society and the economy, and identifies the role, which ILERA might play in this context.

Janice Bellace, from the US, was president - the first female president - between 2009 and 2012. In her chapter, "ILERA: Building on Tradition and Values in Responding to the Challenges of the Information Age," she reflects on ILERA as a sustainable and growing association, and aspects, such as the character and language traditions of ILERA; the name change; and the expansion of ILERA's global membership. On the issue of renewal, she argues that if ILERA holds true to its traditions, mission and global reach, younger scholars and practitioners will see its value and inject new vitality into its work. Furthermore, she discusses some of the challenges related to globalization and the information age and the digital economy.

Evance Kalula from South Africa was President between 2012 and 2015. In his chapter, "ILERA and the Future of Work: Challenges and Opportunities in the Quest for Universal Decent Work and Social Solidarity," he explores a number of challenges and opportunities, such as labour market regulation; social protection; unemployment; and migration, and uses Africa as a proxy of global concerns. He also discusses future measures to strengthen ILERA, and emphasizes, for example, the importance of including younger scholars and professionals; developing networks and collaboration; strengthening the ILO partnership; and extending ILERA's global membership.

Dong-One Kim from the Republic of Korea was President between 2015 and 2018. The starting point of his concluding chapter, "Conclusion: Exploring Strategies for Labour and Employment Relations as an Academic Field," is the debate on the turmoil and relevance of the field of labour and employment relations, given decreasing union density and collective bargaining coverage in many countries. He examines, through a study of abstracts in major labour and employment relations journals in the period between 1947 and 2014, how researchers in the field have responded to and discussed strategic options and future implications for the field. The study implies that the field has evolved, but maintained its core (i.e. union-related topics). New phenomena and realities have been embraced, and the field orientation has shifted from economics to management; from state to market; and from collective labour to individual employees. Kim concludes by arguing for the expansion and revitalization of the field of labour and employment relations, and for the incorporation of emerging trends, such as the gig-economy; AI and the Fourth Industrial Revolution; emerging alternative representative bodies; and new forms of labour disputes.

Concluding Remarks and a Future Outlook

The past-presidents' chapters offer rich and multifaceted perspectives on the development of ILERA and the field of labour and employment relations, as well as inspiring ideas on the future direction. One common theme is the need to creatively, critically and constructively engage with the profound change and transformation that affects both the world of work and labour markets and our field of research. Another common theme is a great commitment to ILERA and a belief in the association's resilience, multitude and innovation.

In moving forward, we are able to build on ILERA's traditions, strengths and dynamics, and in this context, I believe three aspects are worth highlighting, namely, societal challenges and policy development; internationalization and inclusion; and, interdisciplinary collaboration.

ILERA - and research and higher education in the evolving field of labour and employment relations - has a key role to play in addressing global societal challenges, such as sustainable development; employment and decent work; poverty and inequality; aging populations and intergenerational tension; technological change, digitalization and AI; migration, and, climate change. Here, ILERA benefits from its tradition of bringing together scholars, social partners, practitioners, governments and policy makers, and from its long-standing and close collaboration with the ILO.

ILERA is by nature and ideology global and international. Research, and the work and engagement of scholars, is guided by global academic values, such as academic freedom, openness, inclusion, transparency, collegiality and curiosity. It is important to continue to extend the global reach and relevance of ILERA, to welcome new members into our community and to further comparative perspectives.

It is also crucial, from the perspective of legitimacy and high quality, to promote gender equality and diversity within ILERA, at all levels and activities. Furthermore, along the lines of inclusion, ILERA can serve as a vital platform for exchange and collaboration between scholars at different stages of their careers, and assist in mentoring early career researchers and highlighting their contributions.

There is an increasing awareness, by universities, governments and international organizations, of the need for interdisciplinary research, both when it comes to making ground-breaking discoveries and to successfully addressing societal challenges. ILERA - and the field of labour and employment relations - is already one-step ahead, as it has always crossed disciplinary boundaries, and facilitated a multifaceted study of the world of work. ILERA - and the world and regional congresses - can contribute to dynamic innovation in theories, methodologies and data collection in our field, and further stimulate the exploration of intersections between the field of labour and employment relations and other disciplinary fields.

In conclusion, as the current President of ILERA I am happy, honored and humble to follow in the footsteps of these past-presidents, and to host the next, 19th, ILERA World Congress in Lund in Sweden, on June 21-24, 2021 on the theme of "Making and Breaking Boundaries in Work and Employment Relations."

Notes

1 On the history of ILERA, see Kaufman, B.E. (2004) *The Global Evolution of Industrial Relations. Events, Ideas and the IIRA*, International Labour Office.

2 See the ILERA website https://www.ilo.org/public/english/iira/index.htm.

References

Kaufman, B.E. (2004) *The Global Evolution of Industrial Relations. Events, Ideas and the IIRA*, International Labour Office.

My Experience with the IIRA (ILERA)

Friedrich Furstenberg

02

Personal Background

Originally the International Industrial Relations Association (IIRA) was founded as an association of country-based academic institutes as well as related researchers. I belong to the initially small group of post-war social scientists occupied with empirical research in the field of industrial relations. In 1951, I wrote my diploma thesis on a theoretical analysis of trade union demands. Based upon a Fulbright grant, in 1953/54 I was member of the Human Relations Research Group located at the New York State School of Industrial Relations, affiliated to Cornell University in Ithaca, New York. Under the leadership of William Foote Whyte I was also engaged in research and contributed to his well-known book Money and Motivation, which he edited in 1955. During my stay in 1957 as researcher at the London School of Economics I became well acquainted with Ben Roberts, the later founder of the IIRA. He was my adviser when I studied both joint consultation in the civil airport industry and later the establishment of a general wage structure in British coal mining. Before being appointed university professor I worked at the Daimler-Benz Corporation as superintendent of the central training department and was given a profound insight into the praxis and problems of Human Resource Management. My international experience was augmented by field studies of industrial relations and management structures in large Japanese corporations 1965-1970 as well as by continuous field research and teaching in both the Federal Republic of Germany and in Austria. Through my stay as Visiting Professor in Sydney I came into close contact with John Niland and Russell Lansbury. In 1984 I participated in a conference held in Sydney and sponsored by the Hancock Committee to discuss alternatives for the Australian system of arbitration in industrial relations. Through François Sellier I acquired contact with the French Laboratoire d'économie et de sociologie du travail (LEST) in Aix en Provence and acted as Supervisory Board member. My research contacts abroad provided the establishment of closer personal relations with experts in these countries who later held offices in the IIRA and even became its presidents.

Soon after the establishment of the IIRA, being at that time professor for sociology at the University of Linz, I succeeded 1967 in founding the soon IIRA-affiliated Austrian Research Association for Labour Relations. Also in 1967 we had a European meeting of IIRA members, a forerunner of the IIRA European regional congresses. Since then I acted as member of the Executive Committee. I also participated regularly in the World Congresses and contributed original papers.

Focus of IIRA Activities

Main organizational features determined the range of early IIRA activities: the understanding of industrial relations as a multidisciplinary field, open for scientific inquiry, its international scope and administrative affiliation with the International Labour Office (ILO) in Geneva, which provides secretariat and location.

The dominant Anglo-Saxon influence as starting point of IIRA activities fostered an approach centered upon union-management bargaining and opened a broad multidisciplinary perspective of underlying phenomena. In Europe this approach was traditionally limited by departmental boundaries in universities and governmental administration. However, the actual technical, economic and social processes shaping the structures of work, the interactions between workers and management as well as the orientations and intentions of the actors involved reflect all dimensions of social life. The conferences of the IIRA contributed much to broaden an integrating view. Likewise important is the dominating science-based, objective presentation of facts and their discussion, countervailing the ideological manifestations in political arenas.

Like the ILO, the IIRA and the succeeding International Labour and Employment Relations Association (ILERA) are marked by providing an open international platform without prejudice for all participants adhering to the Charter of the United Nations. Thus the activities of the IIRA (ILERA) promote understanding of basic issues in nations, regions and organizations with different socio-economic standards, including a global perspective.

Administrative basis of IIRA (ILERA) operations is the affiliation with the ILO. A senior ILO official normally conducts and supervises ongoing activities. This opens access to the worldwide available organizational resources of the ILO which augments IIRA (ILERA) activities with programs and policy issues and which as a counter-move provides an international network of scholars.

As an IIRA president I cooperated closely with Alfred Pankert and Alan Gladstone who acted as secretaries during that time. Without their fundamental administrative knowledge and aptitude based upon an international network my presidential activities would have been wasted effort.

Survey of My Contributions

For a long range of years the focus of my activities related to the IIRA has been consultations within the Executive Committee. There the planning and execution of IIRA programs has been discussed thoroughly, a major focus being the preparation of World Congresses with a triannual sequence and increasingly of regional congresses.

I also participated in informal consultations, mainly organized by the Industrial Relations and Labour Administration Department of the ILO. As an example, I give a survey of my statement from October 1985 on the future of industrial relations in industrialized market economies.

As a starting point I referred to the broader context of future trends: general processes of social change, adaptation processes, margins for autonomous innovation and perhaps social reform. I laid my focus upon the main factors determining an industrial relations system: structure of the labour market, social structure and orientation of actors concerned, including policy statements, and the institutional framework, including governmental regulation.

Concerning future trends in labour markets in advanced economies, I referred to observations of an increasing participation, especially women, and a decreasing participation period for major groups of employees, mainly due to prolonged education and training as well as periods of unemployment and provisions for early pensioning. A growing trend toward administered and segmented labour markets could be observed, which affects individual choice and widens the gap between "central" and "peripheral" employment. Likewise was observed an increasing instability of work structures, marked by change of job contents, worker transfer and multiple jobs, all requiring greater flexibility. Besides, the aging process of the population in some advanced countries was accompanied by population pressure from less developed countries, resulting in increased migration.

All these trends had to be seen against the secular phenomenon of differential development of labour productivity, causing a shift of the labour force toward service operations, mainly containing information handling and processing. Limitational factors affecting economic growth rates made some structural unemployment unavoidable.

I referred to the fact that industrial relations systems are mainly affected by changes in the relative autonomy of bargaining partners, the levels and contents of bargaining, and the augmentation of bargaining procedures by additional problem solving participation. I pointed at the trend toward "antagonistic cooperation," marked by the willingness to participate in joint problem solving without losing the identity based upon basic interests.

At that time (1985), future trends in my view were marked by a dilemma in structural adjustment: the growing bureaucratization and interdependence of large-scale processes resulted in centralization, oligarchic guidance and rather strict control of spontaneity. On the other hand, the growing complexity of labour-market processes called for greater flexibility. Besides, trade union member consensus often is based upon spontaneous expression of demands and relevant action. As powerful movements try to avoid falling back to only locally operating groups it appeared likely that unions would become more flexible both in their organizational structure and in their strategy. Government is not only setting a normative framework but is a major partner in the system as employer in the public sector. Modern democratic governments will rather refrain from direct interference in the industrial relations system. An alternative is tripartite participation.

Perhaps my main contribution to the further development of the IIRA organization has been as incoming president at the 6th World Congress in Kyoto 1983 and my initiative to establish IIRA Study Groups, originally called "working groups." Members of the IIRA were invited to form such groups to pursue specific research topics. An initial approval by the Executive Committee was needed. Soon six groups were formed, organized by such prominent chairpersons as Jack Barbash, Roger Blanpain, Dorothea Gaudard, the Yougoslav Grozdanic, Tadashi Hanami and Tiziano Treu, three of them later becoming IIRA presidents. The number of study groups grew steadily. They did not only develop as important networks for continuous scientific communication. They also produced numerous publications. But perhaps even more important is the fact, that these study groups provide the IIRA (ILERA) with an infrastructure which opens constant participation beyond the multinational congresses. My remarkably successful proposal was appreciated and later an award was given to me at the 10th World Congress.

After my nomination 1983 as president-elect I prepared actively the agenda of the forthcoming World Congress 1986 in Hamburg. The main topics were technological change and labour relations, industrial forms of workers' participation with special reference to the Federal Republic of Germany, new trends in working-time arrangements, cooperation and conflict in public service labour relations, and labour relations as a strategic factor in development. As may be observed, the program did not concentrate entirely upon the classical bargaining issues but included already as well themes related to labour and employment relations below and besides the industrial bargaining level. But the arising transnational negotiations and regulations still remained less noticed.

My presidential address was devoted to the topic "Societal structural change and the developmental potential of industrial relations": Industrial relations can be recognized as a field with sequences of strategic actions in situations of conflict, confrontation or competition. They are interest-oriented and geared to specific goals. Four classes of objectives and decisions are distinguished: economic benefit, political power and influence, social status, and instrumental efficiency. Their rationalization does not evolve automatically and cannot be manipulated at will. Procedures for cooperation must be established. The capacity for regulation depends on the applicability, consistency and acceptance of the solutions found. Innovative trends relating to both goals and tools are: participatory standard setting procedures, the ongoing process of information, consultation and decision-taking, a complex field of action, concerning the total life sphere of the workers and their dependants and a non-discriminatory application of rules and agreements. But the expansion of industrial relations has also created problems: broadened participation makes consensus more difficult, new areas lead to competition with other social interest groups and call for new types of cooperation, and increased regulation requires corresponding organizational infrastructures. Industrial relations can only be successful if they set standards which are both socially and culturally acceptable, thereby enhancing the quality of life at work.

Retrospective Orientation Toward the Future

Due to my long affiliation with the IIRA, also as an individual member, I try to observe the development of ILERA issues as they manifest themselves, increasingly from a global perspective, in the topics of world and regional congresses and study groups. They reflect trends both in policies and in structural change of employment and labour relations. Impacts emerging from problem areas influence especially their framework of activity (regulatory patterns and their extent), the characteristics of the parties involved (actors), the actions they pursue, the current areas of activity as well as their room for maneuver and strategies.

According to the interdisciplinary quality of labour and employment relations as a research field, attention must be given to a possible tendency that a specific scientific background might dominate the perspective. Then instead of analyzing the impact of structures and systems upon employment and labour relations exclusive self-reference to juridical, economic or social patterns of thought could take place.

The survey of my experience leads me to conclusions concerning the future scope of ILERA activities. The traditional starting point for research has been an examination of the structure and activities of labour-market partners conducting collective negotiations and contracting agreements, and of ways of governmental interference including the emerging legislative framework. In this way a path dependency for research was established that aims at the analysis of relevant established societal institutions and of corresponding practices. However, the international spread of labour markets with representative bodies for negotiations, increasingly connected with transnational networks, and a trend toward flexibilization and individualized agreements have enlarged the issues of concern.

Changes in Labour Force

A topic of constant attention has been *changes in the labour force*, both qualitative and quantitative, with special concern to the rate and shape of female participation. In economically advanced countries the integration of women in the labour market has been achieved, however, with the particular features of widespread part-time work and breaks in working careers. It can also be noted that there has been only partial alignment with the social status of men. Wage inequality and the problem of the double burden of family (childcare) and job remain unsolved issues. The necessary and stable integration of women in the labour process cannot be achieved with temporary contracts and temporary work. Integration will need to be focused on regular labour contracts and the reduction of the double burden. This will have consequences: in the criteria of work allocation, career design and in adjustments to wage structure and interest representation. Fundamental disparities between the requirements of work and family life, the quality of leisure time and social participation must be avoided. The aging process within the population will accelerate. This will present the challenge of finding adequate and productive work for older cohorts, while at the same time being aware of the necessity for sufficient retirement provision.

Labour-market Structures and Processes

A central focus of observations and research always have been *labour-market structures and processes*, the obstacles included which lead to reduced participation of persons or groups willing to work. The concept of marginality of problem groups appeared to be useful to deal with conditions of low or irregular participation in the labour market. Likewise, structural change (e.g. increasing segmentation) due to external factors (differential modernization, employment by transnationally operating enterprises, development of high-technology sectors, business cycles) is observed. Special attention always was given to the development of work conditions in the informal or low union-organized sectors of labour markets. The qualification structures of the labour force have drastically changed as a consequence of technological innovations, in particular the introduction and dissemination of information and communication technology, so that traditional forms of work are being put into question. A partial exclusion of low-qualified workers from the labour market can be observed. The pronounced differences between the core workforce on the one side and the employees with fixed-term contracts, part-time workers and temporary agency workers on the other side indicate a dual labour-market structure with two types of labour relations: "central" and "peripheral." When applying this typology it must be taken into consideration that the labour-market segmentation corresponds to the characteristics of the relevant employee group. They are marked mainly by gender, country of origin, age and work disabilities. These groups often reflect a bias in the employment practice of the potential employer, particularly noticeable within the buffer segment of the labour market. It has also to be considered that the allocation of workers is not done only according to social standards.

Employment Policies

Another wide range of analyses are *employment policies* both at macro- (national and regional) and micro-levels (enterprise, plant). Patterns of remuneration, recruitment, training and promotion and their impact upon employment chances provide themes for presentation at the congress level.

In practice, wage and salary differentials vary according to the degree of standardization of performance. The clearer this is, the more it is possible to empirically ascertain the level of difficulty of the work through classification in collectively agreed remuneration scales. Work performance is increasingly systemically linked and only calculated individually in a limited way. This does however apply more to work with an intermediate level of performance. Non-standard fields of highly skilled qualifications justify "individualization", which is very difficult to find a norm for in collective agreements. The consequence is an extension to collective regulations through individual agreements.

It is seen that changes in the organization of work have far-reaching consequences for the employee in the structuring of tasks. The increasing application of information and communication technology and the relative growth in the high-tech sector is accompanied by a growing intellectualization of work assignments which are subject to constant change. The necessary knowledge for the ongoing rationalization of work processes becomes obsolete as they become successful. It is no longer "know-how" that is accumulated as a form of lifelong working capital, but it is rather the dependence on a continuing learning process. For the organization of work the result is the identification of new segmentation between the qualified and highly motivated core workforce with the ability to adjust to ever-changing challenges and the rather immobile group of employees with intermediate qualifications and levels of motivation that are dependent on routine training and instructions.

The organization of work in projects is becoming widespread, with a tendency to outsource and a formation of cross-organization networks. Exemplary in this respect is the spread of multi-functioning teams engaged in planning and operations involving highly technical equipment. In larger projects they become semi-independent operational units in expanded cross-organization networks. Their social climate is characterized by the necessity for cooperation and competition at the same time. Members of the team with below average performance will tend to be excluded. Basically these multi-functional teams are linked to work on a contract basis and in the long-term are therefore unstable. As they change projects the composition of the teams changes.

This leads to a second segmentation process: between stable and transitory operations. At the level of higher qualifications a gradual change in the employee status can be observed, in a shift to the risky status of the self-employed and in addition, to the fixed-term employment of experts. In this context, individually negotiated contracts are possible. At the level of fewer qualifications an expansion of atypical employment relations can be identified. They are characterized by fixed-term contracts for unskilled and temporary work. The consequences are unstable employment relationships and working careers.

Significance of Qualification Problems

The fundamental *significance of qualification problems* for labour relations becomes clear. A possible devaluation of qualification affects the basis of job-related self-assessment. Experiences of recent years in Germany point to significant weaknesses in the regulatory competence of the social partners.

First of all, it is necessary to support application-oriented qualifications and competence and to maintain this potential, not only through training but also by promoting initiative and individual learning. Therefore, both material and non-material incentives are needed, which are situation-specific and differentiated according to age, gender and the life situation. The general aim to reduce the reservoir of the unskilled through general education and indiscriminate vocational training is often insufficient and leads to dead ends in view of the actually given placement chances. That is followed by expensive and time consuming re-training measures.

On the other hand, there is a necessity to set up a system of lifelong learning, also in combination with career planning that offers an individual development perspective. This has more to do with developing competences according to the needs of the market and the life situation than the acquisition of formal vocational training certificates. Therefore, education centers can be re-structured to become placement centers for low-wage jobs if learning success and opportunities have been put into question.

Organization Patterns of Interest Representations in the Labour Market

Organization patterns of interest representations in the labour market with their basic impact upon industrial relations are of permanent concern. The variety of their appearance, e.g. company unions versus industrial or craft unions, and in view of the main trend of diminishing union power, legal forms of interest presentation or even informal modes are observed and discussed.

An example is given by the development in Germany. The focus of action of the employer associations has traditionally been the collective negotiations with the trade unions after consultation with the member companies, and in the administration of the achieved collective agreements, with the support from the large-scale industries as a decisive element. Sectoral collective agreements with generally binding clauses covering the normal regional conditions for labour relations have been eroding since the mid-1990s. Company-related special regulations and opening clauses for core areas of collectively agreed regulations (collective agreement with flexible working-time agreements and collectively agreed norms with lower measures for employment security) become usual. An orientation to the often heterogeneous interests of the member companies gains priority over a strengthening of the bargaining position with the trade unions. One indicator is the increase in the number of parallel employer associations without collective agreement coverage (OT associations) - above all in the small- and medium-sized business sector.

The trade unions are subject to long-term membership decline in the same way as the employer associations. A reduction in the collective power to design and implement agreements can be seen in the decline in collective agreements and in the decentralization of industrial relations. For the trade unions a reason for this structural weakness is changes in the composition of the workforce: the increasing proportion of women and employees in the service sector, as well as a decrease in the amount of full-time employment. There are also indications of a change in orientation among younger employees, which is associated with the decline of the traditional "working culture" and a turning away from ideological trade union positions. These indications are not, however, a complete explanation. But the membership erosion, above all in the small- and medium-sized enterprises and the change in the social milieu among the workforce are clear obstacles to the new recruitment of members. The long-lasting development of the trade unions, including multi-branch associations, has been replaced by a significant trend toward differentiation. It can be seen in the emergence of branch trade unions with a stronger membership based on vocational orientation.

Contents and Structures of Negotiations

Other key areas are changes in the contents and structure of negotiations, related to both internal and external challenges, mainly political, economic and technological trends. The predominant orientation of interest representations in the context of labour relations can be characterized as the striving for power to design and implement ideas, conservation of the organizational setup, achievement of targets and the purpose of maintaining acceptance of conformity with regulations. Socio-cultural traditions have led to an entrenchment of visions which ideologically have the function of integration - or of limitation. Their significance is diminishing. Of fundamental significance in some countries is the assumption of an insurmountable conflict of the contrasts of "capital" and "work," which in a weakened form are seen in industrial relations to continue as the contrasts of "conflict partnership" and "social partnership." But in fact the employer and employee are dependent on each other for the achievement of their aims, so that in the event of conflicts there is wide scope for amicably negotiated solutions. In addition, a tendency toward welfare state structures offers a widespread participation in the planning, execution and monitoring of all the societal fields of activity which affect the interests of the workforce. There the presence of the social partners on supervisory boards is guaranteed - often with tripartite, equal representation - in the monitoring of social institutions and also in commissions for the preparation and execution of socio-political programs. However, the decrease in binding collective agreements on working conditions has noticeably reduced their regulatory competence. As a consequence special attention is given to ways and means of governmental interference, by law, decree, "persuasion" or indirectly by economic and social policy.

Additional Arrangements for Nation-state Regulatory Patterns

The progressive formation of transnational economic and social areas is leading to *additional arrangements for nation-state regulatory patterns.* An example is the form of a social dialogue, which is increasingly taking place in the European Community: the setting up of European works councils, the social dialogue between umbrella organizations at European level and the well-designed European Employment Strategy.

Possible Guiding Principles for the Future

Main prospective ideas are incorporated in the global demand for "decent work," pronounced 1999 by the ILO. In this term the endeavors of the working population are summarized, covering the chance to have a productive occupation, a fair income, workplace security and social protection for the family, improved opportunities for personal advancement and social integration, freedom of speech, participation in all decisions of vital importance, as well as equality for men and women. Within the framework of flexible forms of work, which presuppose increased education, intrinsic motivation, initiative and more cooperation in the economic value chain process, these fundamental areas of interest and the associated subjective aspirations become more valid. It remains open to what extent the form of organized interests will be realized, and at what levels action will be taken. But, labour and employment relations will furthermore take a pre-eminent role in the achievement of possible advances.

Bibliography

Fuerstenberg, Friedrich (1991) *Structure and Strategy in Industrial Relations,* Bulletin of Comparative Labour Relations 21. Special Issue, 199pp. Deventer.

Kaufmann, Bruce E. (2004) *The Global Evolution of Industrial Relations,* International Labour Office, 722pp.

Times of Change and Deep Transformation: IIRA 9th World Congress, Sydney 1992[1]

John Niland

03

The invitation to pen this essay for the 50th anniversary of the ILERA World Congress in Seoul 2018, offers a welcome opportunity to revisit the themes and experiences from a predecessor event some 25 years earlier: the 9th World Congress in 1992 of the International Industrial Relations Association, in Sydney. It was a time of growing public policy interest in industrial relations in Australia, and elsewhere. It was a time to celebrate the underlying strength of our international body, which I highlighted in my President's Invitation to the Congress:

> The International Industrial Relations Association has matured into one of the leading professional organizations on the international scene and now provides an ideal forum for industrial relations specialists from all around the world to meet one another and maintain contact in the spirit of exchanging ideas and exploring research outcomes. Our strength and standing comes from the membership base - 30 country members from every continent, 44 affiliated research institutes and over 1,200 individual associate members from some 80 countries. In the past six years, we have sponsored seven regional Congresses in Asia, Europe, the Americas and Africa and two World Congresses in Hamburg (1986) and Brussels (1989). There are now 12 special study groups, with

> several more forming, to encourage scholarly exchange and further research. It is from this impressive background that we come into the Ninth World Congress.
>
> (IIRA, 1992)

But it was also a time of some apprehension about the future. Indeed, the five themes adopted for Sydney, the first of our congresses to be held in the Southern Hemisphere, all picked up, one way or another, a change and transformation narrative:

1. The changing role of the State in industrial relations
2. Trade unions and the future
3. Human resource management and industrial relations
4. Industrial relations and political transformation
5. Labour market policy and practices.

The dominant idea was that decade to decade, perhaps even year to year, things would be different, sometimes profoundly so. These shifting sands impacted not just the key issues in industrial relations, but bore in on the very concept of industrial relations as a cognate area of study, and as a standalone discipline in scholarly endeavor. There were, to be sure, earlier signs that the future would not be what it used to be. Brown, at the 1989 Brussels World Congress, argued that:

> There was once a time when the study of industrial relations was inextricably linked with the study of male, organised manual workers with fulltime, more or less secure, employment. It was not that other categories of labour were not to be found, but they were rarely either sizeable or assertive enough to arouse the concern of policy makers, and the interest of academics …. The workforce is undergoing a major period of change. There are

changes in the sort of people who make it up, and there are changes in what they are being asked to do and the terms on which they are being asked to do it.

(Brown, Brussels, 1989: 3)

In the case of Australia, which I discuss in more detail later, emerging pressures for change were also highlighted at Brussels:

··· while it is the employer's interests that have been the major source of pressure for labour flexibility, it is the key union leaders who have developed the actual strategy determining the nature of Australia's response. They have also been able to exercise considerable influence over the timing and pace of change. Australia has sought to cope with the variety of economic and other pressures by encouraging workplace flexibility within a centralised system - the administered flexibility model.

(Niland and Spooner, 1989: 113)

By the time we arrived at Sydney in 1992, the feeling of challenging change and deep transformation had become palpable. As Bellace observed:

··· it is a natural consequence that structures regulating a disappearing labour market must change. The movement for equal pay for equal value, laws prohibiting sex and age discrimination, and parental leave reflect the change in the labour market. In the area of sex and age, we have a glimpse of the changes that will come in the organization of work and the labour market. They will inevitably change industrial relations, but there is no doubt that the state will be called upon to act in response to these changes.

(Bellace, 1994: 38)

In a salute to our hosts here in Seoul in July 2018, I also note Park's assessment, back then, of the need for change in South Korea:

> … the future of the Korean economy depends on whether unions, management and the government can successfully develop a social contract in a joint effort toward up-market restructuring of the whole economy, as well as the modernisation of industrial relations. If the three actors can succeed in working together, then Korea will soon enter into a stage of more advanced industrialization.
>
> (Park, 1994: 92)

Over half the papers presented 25 years ago were titled to capture the sense of movements afoot in our field of study and practice, and this theme was addressed one way or the other in virtually every paper.

To be more specific, some of the most significant areas addressed on change and transformation were:

1. the declining fortunes of trade union and, indeed, the very question of survival (at least in any meaningful sense);
2. the role of the State in the preservation and promotion of free collective bargaining;
3. emerging globalization as a force for change in industrial relations;
4. the role of industrial relation institutions in political transformation;
5. changing concepts of work in the face of new technologies;
6. trade unions and management as facilitators and/or blockers of change;
7. decentralization of industrial relations processes and the pursuit of lower centers of gravity;
8. the emergence of Human Resources Management (HRM) theory and practice to threaten the status quo and set up the challenge of a

paradigm shift;
9. the role of comparative international industrial relations: how, when and with what effect can lessons be transferred from country to country;
10. strategies to engineer change, or to confound it.

Now, 25 years later, I will endeavor to give the modern reader a feel for the tone and tenor of those transformative times, and what unfolded. My primary source here are the papers presented in 1992, including my own President's Address, all published in the Conference volume (Niland, Lansbury and Verevis, 1994).

To my mind, three areas had special significance, and drew most attention, one way or another: the fate of trade unionism; the future of industrial relations as a field of study; and the related threat/opportunity posed by the rise of HRM. This is where the Congress buzz was to be found. And so, in the final section of this chapter, I discuss the idea that from that buzz the World Congress became a change agent itself, with impact on the big debate of the 1980s and 1990s in Australia: arbitration verses bargaining as the primary mode for processing industrial relations.

This is where the Congress left its mark on the host country; partly through the many papers showcasing the international trend toward decentralization and bargaining modes of operation, but also in showing that change is "normal" and that public policy debate can and does lead to deep transformation of how industrial relations operates.

Trade Unions and the Future

Perceptions at the time of Sydney 1992 were that trade unionism had a survival task at hand. Several quotes illustrate this:

> The sharp decline in union density, which has been experienced in many developed market economies during the past decade in particular, has caused the union movement to reconsider its role and even its future viability. Ben-Israel and Fisher (1992) warn that unions in many countries are engaged in a struggle for survival, and that their future will be determined by their ability to influence the policies adopted by employers and governments, as well as their success in convincing workers to join and remain in their ranks.
>
> (Lansbury and Verevis, 1994: 6)

> Unions face an enormous challenge. Their task, in often difficult economic and political circumstances, is to demonstrate their relevance to members and potential members. This requires a balanced response, with attention devoted to national industry and workplace levels. The penalty for indifference and inaction will be further decline. Our societies will be poorer.
>
> (Davis, 1994: 132)

> The union movement in countries such as France and the United States is no doubt in trouble … At a time when regulation is highly suspect and individualism and market orientations are a la mode, the classic union profile is less attractive … (but not so in Sweden, Finland and Denmark).
>
> (Hammarström, 1994: 159)

It was well known at the time, as is in the present day, that the fate of trade unions rests on many factors. New technology, emphasizing much tighter orbits of control and small-scale production efficiencies in the 1980s and 1990s was changing the face of industrial relations by guaranteeing the decentralized unit a crucial role. As the patterns of basic production change, a transformed industry mix in favor of service and finance and away from manufacturing, were affecting basic industrial relations. Also impacting the world of unionism were customer-dedicated production runs; subcontracted outwork; the rise of a much better educated workforce, which is more inclined to insist on decision-making closer to home; and the general drift toward white-collar work. These are all issues largely beyond the control of trade unions. But they are also issues, in retrospect, that seem less daunting than the pressures coming from today's gig economies and 24/7 news cycles. But more of that later.

In the 1990s, we begin to see that another major challenge to trade unions will be the growing inclination of public opinion to mobilize against what are seen, rightly or wrongly, as indulgent and self-serving stances. Delamotte referred to the impact of French public opinion in forcing public sector unions, particularly in electricity and railways, to modify action that disrupts social and economic life (Delamotte, 1991: 109). The issue, however, runs deeper than just overt industrial conflict. As the OECD itself noted, "unions representing relatively small groups of workers, often enjoying regulatory job protection, have pressed wage claims with little regard for the cost in terms of employment opportunities for others" (Niland, 1994: 460). While this may be more typical of countries with the fragmented bargaining model, such elements also exist elsewhere. How trade unions handle the issues of dual labour markets, internal versus external orbits of job opportunity and the rise of precarious employment would bear heavily on future public perceptions of trade unions. Lessons from the experience of other countries were seen to be increasingly important.

In some countries, like Germany and Australia, the force of constitutional provisions and the general regulatory framework provide a degree of protection from employers and governments that might wish to tap public opinion to exert leverage on trade unions and weaken their standing. But even here, as in countries such as the United States, France and the United Kingdom, where unions lack such protective infrastructure, their fate throughout the 1990s and beyond will be tied to how hard-line they are in trying to preserve (even enhance) the benefits and protections of core workers over those in the peripheral labour force. The fact that women are heavily concentrated in this latter group, and that awareness was growing over equal employment opportunity (EEO) values and practices, reinforced the seriousness of the challenges to be mounted against old-style unionism. It is also worth noting that no set of ideas had a greater impact on work relationships in the 1980s and 1990s than those of EEO, and they have for the most part been internationally generated.

One area where unions did seem able to help shape their future lay in their strategic response to the growing emphasis on enterprise bargaining. Tensions between full-time officials operating at an industry or national level, and the lay officials or unionized worker representatives based within the enterprise were evident in a number of countries (Niland and Clarke, 1991). The leadership challenge was to both decentralize the power and authority needed to bargain at enterprise levels, and centralize the provisions of staff expertise and other resources needed to develop long-run strategies and advise local union entities on the increasingly complex array of technical, economic and organizational issues that confront labour. How this is eventually settled in each case would say much about the likely future relevance of trade unions in modern industrial (and post-industrial) society. I return to this later in the final section on the Congress being a change agent itself.

Also seen as important at the time was whether management's bonding strategies simply seek to move full-time officials to an arm's-length relationship - or will they seek to engineer their complete demise? As Kochan and Wever (1991: 52) saw it, the more trade unions "cling to their traditional roles within the New Deal system, the more freedom and incentives management will have to pursue a union-avoidance strategy." The alternative, taking Germany as an example, is for unions to provide management with assets they would find hard to generate on their own, such as "worker commitment, willingness to undergo training and retraining, governable organizational flexibility at the workplace and active support for structural change." To Streeck (1991: 87), a credible offer of cooperation will reduce the attraction to employers of a test of strength, "even if this means foregoing present opportunities to restore managerial privilege and, in the longer run, deunionize important segments of the labour force." Where unions must have some concern would be the management strategy of cooperation up to the point of relative advantage, and then a switch to a tougher stance to drive home an absolute advantage.

The general picture in the early 1990s, then, was that management could be expected to bolster the trend toward decentralization of industrial relations processes, and this would be enhanced if unions chose to cooperate with an enterprise focus. The scope for more sophisticated strategy development and cautious action had become quite significant, at least to the new unionism. As we are reminded in the classic prisoner's dilemma, by choosing cooperation with one another, unions and management could both be better off in the long run, although an antagonistic posture could well have an even better pay-off for the initiator over the short run. Or not.

All this, viewed from the early 1990s, was at the beginning of the journey from the second to the third industrial revolution. Now, 25 years later, the pace of change is even greater than evident back then, as today we move into the Fourth Industrial Revolution. Yet even with a growing alertness to the concept that change was all around, who in 1992 could have imagined we were headed to a headline last year in the Sydney media: "Young Tech Dudes are Decentralising Unions with Blockchain and AI" (Marin-Guzman, 2017).

The Future of Industrial Relations

As I observed in my President's Address to the 1992 Congress, fields of study and research exist almost always because they have a home within universities, although the academic discipline may be organized differently from country to country. In countries such as Britain, the United States, Australia, Canada and New Zealand (all English-speaking), we find separate departments of industrial relations (at least in the early 1990s). In Europe, industrial relations was more likely to be embodied within the cognate disciplines of economics, politics, law, psychology, sociology and so on. Irrespective of its particular organizational form, the discipline will survive only if it is able to generate or garner sufficient resources, which in turn depends on student demand and on institutional politics, which themselves can be influenced by the moral and financial support coming from practitioners. In this respect the survival of industrial relations as a field of study is no less prosaic than that of music or mathematics, accounting or astronomy, or physics and physiotherapy. In the case of Australia, the development of the academic discipline could be traced through three phases; elements of which were no doubt evident in many other countries.

First, the *foundation phase* ran through the 1950s and 1960s. Academics who had been appointed to the cognate disciplines began to explore the industrial relations issues in their field, to produce such subjects as industrial psychology, labour law, labour history, labour economics and the like. Searching for a special identity, and often feeling marginalized from their own disciplinary mainstream, these academics sought to form distinct institutional groupings. Their efforts were bolstered by a growing interest among students and were supported by industry in specifically focused industrial relations programs. The key professional body, the Industrial Relations Society, emerged in this period and started to become a major force in sustaining the discipline through its funding and organizational support for the nascent *Journal of Industrial Relations.* It mattered little that scholars in the more traditional disciplines worried about the lack of a theoretical framework for industrial relations and the absence of a clear body of research literature to support teaching. These would come in the next phase.

Second, the *growth and consolidation phase* ran throughout the 1970s and into the 1980s. During these years the growth in student numbers was quite extraordinary. At the University of New South Wales, for example, the new major in industrial relations enrolled its first 5 students in 1958; 10 students graduated with an industrial relations major in 1972; by 1978 this had grown more than fourfold to 45 (and was to fall back to fewer than 10 by 1990). Schools of industrial relations emerged, usually in close association with faculties of law or economics and, through a surge in research output, a distinctively Australian body of material emerged. Interestingly, some of the cognate disciplines even courted the presence of industrial relations scholars to help boost student numbers (and therefore their own resource base). Special research centers, funded through earmarked grants from government, emerged. From this powerful platform, a number of leaders in the field, academics as well as practitioners and legislators, began to form the strategy that would lead to Sydney being awarded the 9th World Congress in 1992. The discipline may have been in the doldrums in the United States during this period, but for Australia a golden age of sorts had arrived.

It should be acknowledged that this high point for the discipline in Australia probably had as much to do with the industrial relations dramas being reported daily in a press given to hyperbole and colorful detail, as it did with any discovery of a new mother lode of truth to be taught and researched in the groves of academe. And herein probably lies the essence of the challenge later in surviving the paradigm shift posed by HRM, as discussed shortly.

Third, the *challenge and survival phase* presented itself as we entered the 1990s. We then saw an emerging skepticism about the relevance of industrial relations study among its main stakeholders: students, policy-makers, practitioners and funding bodies. The imperative to approach industrial relations through the portals of HRM were, as elsewhere, strong in Australia, and growing.

Viewed from Sydney 1992, the lesson seemed clear: the shape of an academic discipline - indeed its very existence and survival - is intimately bound up with the institutional arrangements for its teaching and research. If the courses are not offered, the students cannot enroll, and the discipline cannot be grown and ideas cannot be transmitted into contemporary practice, nor can they be passed on down through succeeding generations of scholars. Research and the generation of ideas are dependent on sufficient student interest in a discipline (although, from time to time special support may be extended to keep the seed corn alive through a particularly bad patch). Much of this must have been familiar to academics in other countries; reports were quite common of declining interest among students in traditional industrial relations courses, and as Purcell noted, this can spawn interesting survival techniques:

> It has not gone unnoticed in Britain that a number of academic stalwarts of the labour movement now find themselves holding professorships funded by major companies under the title "Human Resource Management." It is industrial relations by another name, like so many textbooks where the 2nd edition is simply retitled, or like the MBA elective in a major British university where numbers were falling until it was retitled "Human Resource Management" with little change of content.
>
> (Purcell, 1994: 203)

But as Purcell (1994), and Storey (1994: 270) too, so clearly demonstrate, there is much more to HRM than a convenient bolthole for the international relations community in tough times.

Surviving the Paradigm Shift

It is a well-accepted wisdom that species survive when they either repel invaders or adapt to changing circumstances. Some courage, and not a little foolhardiness, may be needed to pursue the defensive strategy. The adaptive strategy, in which industrial relations seeks to better integrate itself with the world of human resource management, had growing appeal in the 1990s. A particular proposition advanced at the time was that the relative attractiveness of one approach over the other may have something to do with age. Older academics, those whose careers may have been forged over the years in the industrial relations dimension, feel both that they have more to defend and less to lose with a last-ditch stand. They are also more likely to have a deeper bond with the spirit of trade unionism. The younger academics, with careers still ahead of them, are likely to be much more adaptive.

A related lesson, viewed from Sydney 1992, is that an academic discipline needs clients and mentors. Just how the discipline projects itself to students and to practitioners is crucial and, in the 1990s, this would be bound up with the idea of what Dunn called the root metaphor. Dunn's argument is that the old industrial relations, focusing on trade unions, collective bargaining, strikes and Dunlopian-rule making, applies a trench warfare approach to life - an approach with a "nervous obsession with what 'the other side' is up to … it tends to foster paranoid melodrama … [which] can be discerned on both sides of the left and right poles of industrial relations analysis" (Dunn, 1990: 10). In contrast, the new industrial relations, which is to say the HRM paradigm, is built on what Dunn calls the "becoming metaphor." While this entails "leaving a safe, familiar place … enduring privation, facing temptations and dangers," there is always the hope that the traveler will prevail over the travails and return home safely. This is inherent in the HRM orientation, at least in the 1990s version, where change and hopeful travel prevail. The journey is important, not the end point that tends never to arrive: "Arrival suggests the end of change, whereas the new industrial relations is about perpetual change" (Dunn, 1990: 21). This bears powerfully upon clients and mentors, who are not necessarily fussed about a lack of intellectual rigor or theoretical respectability. More critical is a root metaphor that can sell hope:

> And who can blame the career-orientated student of the 1980s for not wishing to be trained as a managerial trench soldier when human resource management beckons? Worse, who can blame

> them if they identify those of us in the old industrial relations with our metaphor and come to see us as the ones in the trenches, peeping apprehensively over the sandbags as the tanks of the new paradigm roll unheedingly over our barbed wire? Who can blame colleagues in the new paradigm for seeing us as stuck with an idiom that closes off our options and holds us in a labyrinth of our own making, our research preoccupations confined and blinkered by the earthworks around us. Their metaphor is, after all, so much more open, expansive and even heroic.
>
> (Dunn, 1990: 17)

With these thoughts and fears beginning to circulate, it is of little wonder that HRM finds a place on the Congress agenda of Sydney 1992. The first appearance of HRM as a designated track at a World Congress did not go without comment. Lansbury and Verevis (1994: 8) wondered whether its erstwhile absence reflected "ambivalence, if not hostility, with which HRM has been viewed by many industrial relations scholars." Also noting HRM's maiden appearance, Purcell comments:

> This is the first time, I believe, that our association has devoted a congress theme to human resource management. To some this may be welcomed as a timely response to the new agendas for industrial relations evident in most countries. To others it may be a matter of regret indicative of the creeping managerialism that endangers the traditional concern with employers and employees, their collective organizations, and the role of the State.
>
> (Purcell, 1994: 203)

HRM, to many, was the elephant in the Congress Hall, sometimes ignored, often poked and prodded, at other times cajoled into dialogue with industrial relations. Kochan and Dyer saw HRM itself as at a crossroads of sort in the US, which it may or may not navigate successfully. They wondered whether HRM will achieve its own "transformation from Personnel Administration to a truly strategic orientation and contribution." Or, failing this, are "… the voices of human resource managers and professionals in many firms destined to remain buried deep within the managerial hierarchy, pleading for, but only sporadically receiving, the support and commitment of their more powerful managerial brethren" (Kochan and Dyer, 1994: 236).

Storey saw in the UK experience a set of particularly powerful managerial initiatives which "… have involved not only changes to organisational and managerial structures, beliefs and values, but also a whole panoply of measures directed at redrawing the employment relationship" (Storey, 1994: 289).

In Europe, Regini noted a type of Faustian deal for trade unions, in which:

> They are confronted with a systematic division between daily decisions concerning the organisation at work, in which they are invited to participate, and strategic decisions from which they are generally excluded. More generally, employers are ready to consider paying the economic cost for the slower and slightly modified decision-making process that results from union participation, but not to consider the possibility of substantially modifying their decisions.
>
> (Regini, 1994: 269)

However interpreted, HRM was no ordinary new wave, for it had the potential (though not the certainty) to shift dramatically the underlying power bases within the industrial relations discipline. Among academics, concern was that responsibility for industrial relations was moving to the business schools, where a different paradigm operates. Among practitioners the concern was that the devolution approach and the techniques of HRM serve to mainline the industrial relations function, with the importance of line manager growing at the expense of the specialist. I thought:

> It is not being overly dramatic to wonder whether the discipline will survive much beyond the year 2000. If it does, certainly it will look quite different by then, and a change of name would be only part of the story.
>
> (Niland, 1994: 463)

Much water was to pass under the international relations bridge, and by 2010 we see our peak organization's name changed from that of the International Industrial Relations Association (IIRA) to the new International Labour and Employment Relations Association (ILERA) on the basis that:

> Over the years, the association has broadened the scope of subject matter to issues such as the transnational movement of labour, non-standard work, labour market regulation and trade and labour standards, and discrimination in employment. Many felt that there was a need for our name to reflect this new world of work, the broader subject matter and the reality of developing country labour markets. The new name refers to labour to include all those who work, whether in paid employment, self-employment or the care economy.
>
> (ILERA website)

The World Congress as a Change Agent

A World Congress is seen primarily as a platform for the development and exchange of ideas across national borders. This certainly was true of Sydney 1992. My assessment now, some 25 years later, is that the IIRA 9th World Congress carried real impact, given its recurring themes of change and transformation, which coincided with a similar dynamic within the host country itself. From the mid-1980s and into the 1990s Australia was moving into the unfamiliar territory of industrial relations reform. Given our system's remove from the international mainstream in much of the twentieth century, the many papers and dozens of ideas brought in by the Congress became grist for Australia's nascent transformation movement. Brown and Walsh (1994: 387) noted that "most industrialized countries appear to be set firmly on a course of dismantling their industry-wide arrangements and fragmenting their bargaining structures." Dell'Aringa and Lodovici (1994: 389) felt that "bargaining at the firm level is certainly going to have greater weight."

Many countries, perhaps through the emergence of HRM thinking, perhaps for other reasons, were facing, even embracing, a shift toward enterprise arrangements. Lower centers of gravity for industrial relations carried increasing appeal internationally. This did not go unnoticed in the host country.

In Australia, the policy tension was between the historically embedded (centralized) arbitration mode and the new wave (decentralized) enterprise bargaining proposals. At a time of intense policy debate in Australia over these two approaches, hosting the World Congress, with its many hundreds of international participants, was a sublime moment for the reform camp. Eminent legislators and academics, as well as some of the leading industrial players, all spent time, both in formal sessions and on the Congress sidelines, with their overseas counterparts, many of whom saw an enterprise emphasis as normal, or at least as the new normal.

While industrial relations arrangements vary from country to country, and while each has its own special features, the Australian approach of tribunal-based arbitration was deeply unique. How did this come to pass? Briefly put, it is an accident of history, in the sense that the Australian Constitution was being framed in the 1890s at a time of great industrial upheaval. The imperative, understandably, was to secure in the Constitution a provision (s51xxxv) that provided power to the new national government to enact laws to ensure industrial peace, through "conciliation and arbitration for the prevention and settlement of industrial disputes …." In pursuit of what became known as "a new province for law and order," Australia's intricate network of federal and state industrial relations tribunals emerged, with a strong judicial DNA and a consequent belief in several core features: first, that strikes, to all intents and purposes, could be rendered unnecessary (even illegal) because the tribunals would mete out industrial fairness and wage justice; and second, fairness was to be found in wage uniformity across economic sectors and geography, rather than in wage flexibility. More of this shortly.

There is no doubt that the system to emerge from the very early 1900s served Australia well for many decades, posting much that was socially progressive in a country that prized equality and a fair go for all. It was, as Gardner (2008: 33) notes, "one of the major social experiments of a vibrant, young and successful Australia." But it was also true the that by the 1970s, and then with the growing pace of globalization into the 1980s, academics began to debate whether the arbitration system was any longer fit for purpose. With the Australian dollar floated in 1983, and the wind back of tariff protection being widely bruited, centralized arbitration and wage rigidity seemed even more out of touch with economic reality. Our heritage system came to be seen in some quarters as a "curious beast" (Gardner, 2008: 33), the institutional counterpart of such other Australian exotica as the kangaroo and duck billed platypus!

And so the IIRA 9th World Congress arrived in Sydney in the midst of this debate. Importantly, the Congress was supported with organizational and financial resources from the Federal Government and all six State Governments. The Industrial Relations Societies in each State and at the federal level also provided essential, indeed often enthusiastic, backing. Many of our leading opinion makers were closely engaged with the Congress, as was the New South Wales Conservative Government, led by Premier John Fahey and the Federal Labour Government, led by Prime Minister Paul Keating, both of whom attended the IIRA Opening Ceremony on August 31, 1992. This "sponsorship" meant the Sydney Congress held more front page media interest than might normally be the case.

New South Wales had been the first to lead off with major legislation in 1990 enabling enterprise bargaining, following most of the recommendations of the Green Paper of 1989 on Transforming Industrial Relations (Niland, 1989). By applying a green paper process, Fahey had ensured periods of submission taking, consultation and debate. While the initial enterprise bargaining legislation was put in place just prior to the Congress, there were still many minds critical of this policy development, and indeed whether it should be bedded down into an ongoing arrangement. Some were clearly unimpressed by what was unfolding. To Shaw (1992: 5) it was a "new path to conflict." Gittens (1991) spoke of enterprise bargaining as a "snake oil for the national malaise," while to O'Donnell (1991: 203) it was all "a journey up the garden path." Wright feared we were "playing into the hands of the madmen of the extreme left" (1990: 83). Not to be outdone in colourful imagery, I saw enterprise bargaining as "the light on the horizon" (Niland, 2008: 15).

Around this same time the Keating Government at the national level was also exploring a lower center of gravity in industrial processes. In 1992 it introduced enterprise (or agency) bargaining to the Australian Public Service, in line with recommendation of a Review Report, Breaking New Ground (Niland, Brown and Hughes, 1991). Then, also federally, the Industrial Relations Reform Act 1993 passed into law, providing enterprise bargaining with access to an Australia-wide platform. The mold had been broken. Or had it?

A decade or so on, management interests seemed more inclined to see that change could indeed be engineered, arguing that the new regime actually did not go far enough with devolution. And, so in late 2005 the new Conservative Federal Government under John Howard moved, through legislation, to a *WorkChoices* regime. Among other things, it sought to tilt away from collective enterprise agreements toward individual contracts agreed directly between employer and employee. The Howard Government lost the 2007 election (and the Prime Minister his own seat), essentially through a campaign mounted by trade unions against *WorkChoices*, and promoting in its stead the enterprise bargaining model; not, it might be noted, by seeking a return to traditional tribunal arbitration. How things had changed when bargaining of any form no longer is seen as the thin edge of the American wedge!

This shift toward a bargaining mode required more than just the enabling legislation from the Parliament of New South Wales in 1990 and the Australian Parliament in 1993 (as important were the resulting structural frameworks). Progression to stable and mature enterprise bargaining also needed the players to address several of the core values in the Australian industrial relations culture. This is one respect, I would argue, where the "change agent effect" of the 1992 Congress might be discerned, at least in retrospect.

As noted earlier, the culture of tribunal-led arbitration favored outcomes of high uniformity, as befits the judicial DNA. This was embedded in the notion of comparative wage justice which meant that similar jobs paid the same rate irrespective of industry or geographic location. The first key feature of the enterprise bargaining model requiring a shift in the Australian industrial relations culture was to lessen its embrace of uniformity in favor of variability. This would be no mean feat. But we might argue that the growing awareness of international practices, generated by the 9th World Congress, over time helped Australia to make the transition to a more flexible, diversified approach essential for mature enterprise bargaining.

Interestingly, a silver lining to the uniformity cloud emerged: compulsory superannuation for all employees. This idea had first appeared in a macro-level social contract (the Prices and Incomes Accord) between the Australian peak trade union body (ACTU) and the reform minded Federal Labour Government of Bob Hawke, in 1983. What unfolded was that employees would forego a uniform national productivity linked wage increase (initially 3%) which employers would match and pay into a new nationwide superannuation system. Later, as enterprise bargaining took hold, national wage cases faded from the IR landscape, a national productivity element now effectively became available for distribution to all employees though the new compulsory superannuation system. Currently, employers contribute 9.5% of wages to each employee's superannuation account, which is often matched by the individual employee. The end result is that superannuation "savers down under put aside four times as much as their UK counterparts."

The *second key feature* of the enterprise bargaining model which was quite foreign to Australia's industrial relations culture concerned the legal status of strikes. The prevailing outlook at the beginning of the last century was that the "new province for law and order" should mean, in the words of Justice Gallagher, there was no such thing as the "right to strike." This had a perverse effect over time. By imagining that no strikes need occur, society ignores the inevitable and denies itself the ability to inject fundamental stability into the industrial relationship by regulating when certain strikes might occur (and when they cannot). Hence the Niland Green Paper promoted the distinction between interest disputes and rights disputes (however they are termed in the Australian lexicon) and the need to embed this distinction in legislation.

While there were particular conditions and caveats, the essential theme in the Green Paper was that interest disputes (in the first phase of the industrial calendar) should be acknowledged as lawful, but rights disputes (in the second phase) should be unlawful and attract the probability of penalties and sanctions. In their submissions during the period of Green Paper consultation, many employers were unhappy with a recognition that any strike could be legal. And quite a few union commentators opposed the practical limitation in any form, particularly the concomitant need to lay out penalties to operate in the event of breach. Other commentators worried that the tribunals would have to stay their hands even as interest-based strikes became drawn out, with the media and opposition politicians clamoring for an arbitrated solution.

In the end, the New South Wales State Government balked at the "balancing" provision, and the ensuring legislation in 1990 did not embed the right to strike in the first phase of the process (further evidence of the cultural barriers to be overcome). Through time, however, there came an acceptance of the idea that some industrial action would be "protected" while other action be "unprotected" and could draw penalties. In this respect, the federal industrial relations legislation from the mid-1990s better supported the framework for enterprise-level bargaining (after the New South Wales initial legislation got the reform ball rolling). This has helped shift the culture on industrial action in Australia, and in part accounts for the dramatic downward trend in Australian strike activity (which for much or our history was at appallingly high levels).

Conclusion

In this chapter I have taken the opportunity to offer some personal reflections on the Sydney World Congress in 1992. It was a time of great challenges and change, and for the host country itself the beginning of a period of deep transformation. The challenge facing industrial relations was to develop a discipline which is at the one time intellectually satisfying to scholars - something more than the academic equivalent of ambulance chasing - but which is also useful to policy making and to professional practice. These are not incompatible goals. By and large medicine, law, engineering and a host of other fields of study have managed to capture the right symbiosis. Admittedly, there is one aspect that poses a particular challenge for industrial relations, and that is the fact that the major changes in our area - devolution and focusing of energies at the enterprise level - drew more on the skills of the trained "generalist" line manager than on those of the professional "specialist." In one sense, this was at the time the feared face of HRM. But with the interest in change and transformation so evident in the papers and sessions at the 9th World Congress, a way forward could well emerge.

However, as I observed in my President's Address, this would eventuate "only for the new industrial relations, not the old" (Niland, 1994: 468).

For Australia, the 1992 World Congress came along at just the right time to help secure the momentum for our escape from industrial-relations xenophobia. If that is putting it too strongly, as some will no doubt argue, at least we can fairly say the Congress helped give interest in and legitimacy to the international perspective, whose message at the time was primarily one of devolution and decentralization in a globalizing world. We can now note, for example, that the break from centralized arbitration coincided with other important macro policy shifts toward free(er) trade, the rise of an independent central bank and a floating dollar. In this new economic environment Australia began what has now been a record 26 years of continuous economic growth. Without overstating the case, some credit here is fairly given to enterprise bargaining and its more flexible approach to industrial relations. And to the forces that made this possible.

The Australian experience with enterprise bargaining carries several lessons for the study of deep transformation. First, ideas from offshore can and do help shape insights and solutions. The main sight lines should be, for the most part, across national borders, not back through the traditions of a single country. Also important are the agents for change, including events such as an IIRA or ILERA World Congress, where thousands of participants from a hundred or more countries can foster and facilitate a multinational perspective.

Second, looking back over the past 25 years, it is fair to wonder whether in the modern environment any of the key parameters of any system will hold through time. I mentioned the short-lived *WorkChoices* regime as an existential challenge to enterprise bargaining in the mid-2000s. Though a passing phase, at the time it seemed existential enough. Now, in 2018, another strong push to revisit and revise the reforms of the 1990s has appeared. This time, both trade union and management interests are at the ramparts of "traditional" enterprise bargaining, each with the common refrain that the system has been gamed to give the other side excessive power. No doubt changes will be made, particularly to more actively protect vulnerable workers outside the enterprise bargaining framework and to address a seriously deteriorating wage curve, and other issues, thrown up by the surge to the Fourth Industrial Revolution.

Linked to this, a third lesson is that change, even significant change as in the 1990s, itself can accelerate, sometimes with alarming speed. We now talk not just about deep transformation, but about profound disruption, driven through gig effects, and those tech dudes with their blockchain and AI methodologies! So it is probably time for a closer look at whether, after 25 years, the enterprise bargaining system, launched with some help from the buzz at the 9th World Congress, is broken, and in need of repair. Or do we need to move well beyond revised models of bargaining to a whole new paradigm - something which itself was contemplated in 1992. Perhaps what we need in Australia is another World Congress!

Note

1 This chapter was initially prepared for the Former Presidents Session at the 50th Anniversary World Congress of the International Labour and Employment Relations Association (ILERA), July 23-27, 2018, COEX in Seoul, South Korea.

References

Bellace, J. (1994) "The Role of the State in Industrial Relations," in Niland, J., Lansbury, R. and Verevis, C. (eds.), *The Future of Industrial Relations*, Sage Publications, pp. 19-40.

Brown, W. (1989) "Aspirations and Expectations of a New Labour Force and Implications for Industrial Relations," IIRA 8th World Congress Proceedings, Brussels.

Brown, W. and Walsh, J. (1994) "Corporate Policies and the Internationalisation of Markets," in Niland, J., Lansbury, R. and Verevis, C. (eds.), *The Future of Industrial Relations*, Sage Publications, pp. 377-388.

Davis, E. (1994) "Trade Unionism in the Future," in Niland, J., Lansbury, R. and Verevis, C. (eds.), *The Future of Industrial Relations*, Sage Publications pp. 115-134.

Delamotte, Y. (1991) "France," in Niland, J. and Clarke, O. (eds.), *Agenda for Change: An International Analysis of Industrial Relations in Transition*, Allen & Unwin pp. 90-114.

Dell'Aringa, C. and Lodovici, M.S. (1994) "Industrial Relations and labour Policies in European Countries," in Niland, J., Lansbury, R. and Verevis, C. (eds.), *The Future of Industrial Relations*, Sage Publications pp. 389-404.

Dunn, S. (1990) "Root Metaphor in the Old and New Industrial Relations," *British Journal of Industrial Relations*, 28(1), pp. 1-31.

Gardner, M. (2008) "Beyond WorkChoices: Negotiating a Moment," *The Economic and Labour Relations Review*, 18(2), pp. 33-43.

Gittens, R. (1991) "Enterprise Bargaining: The Snake Oil for the National Malaise," *Sydney Morning Herald*, April 27.

Hammarström, O. (1994) "Local and Global: Trade Unions in the

Future," in Niland, J., Lansbury, R. and Verevis, C. (eds.), *The Future of Industrial Relations*, Sage Publications, pp. 152-163.

IIRA (1992) Congress Program, Sydney.

ILERA(2019) Website (www.ilo.org/public/english/iira/html/about/about.htm).

Kochan, T.A. and Dyer, L. (1994) "Managing Transformational Change: The Role of Human Resource Professionals," in Niland, J., Lansbury, R. and Verevis, C. (eds.), *The Future of Industrial Relations*, Sage Publications, pp. 219-238.

Kochan, T.A. and Wever, K.R. (1991) "United States of America," in Niland, J. and Clarke, O. (eds.), *Agenda for Change: An International Analysis of Industrial Relations in Transition*, Allen & Unwin, pp. 19-52.

Lansbury, R.D. and Verevis, C. (1994) "Change and Continuity in Industrial Relations," in Niland, J., Lansbury, R. and Verevis, C. (eds.), *The Future of Industrial Relations*, Sage Publications, pp. 3-13.

Marin-Guzman, D. (2017) "Young Tech Dudes are Decentralising Unions with Blockchain and AI," *Sydney Morning Herald*, December 28.

Niland, J. (1989) *Transforming Industrial Relations in New South Wales - A Green Paper*, NSW Government Printer, Sydney. Vol 1 and Vol 2.

Niland, J. (1994) "Change and the International Exchange of Ideas," in Niland, J., Lansbury, R. and Verevis, C. (eds.), *The Future of Industrial Relations*, Sage Publications, pp. 451-471.

Niland, J. (2008) "The NSW Green Paper Twenty Years On: A Reflection on the Future," *The Economic and Labour Relations Review*, 18(2), pp. 15-22.

Niland, J. and Spooner, K. (1989) "Structural Change and Industrial Relations in Australia," IIRA 8th World Congress Proceedings, Brussels.

Niland, J. and Clarke, O. (1991) *Agenda for Change: An International Analysis of Industrial Relations in Transition*, Allen & Unwin.

Niland, J., Brown, W. and Hughes, B. (1991) *Breaking New Ground: Enterprise, Bargaining and Agency Agreements for the Australian Public Service: A Report Prepared for the Australia Minister of Industrial Relations*, Canberra (141pp).

Niland, J., Lansbury, R. and Verevis, C. (1994) *The Future of Industrial Relations*, Sage Publications.

O'Donnell, V. (1991) "Up the Garden Path? Enterprise Bargaining and Decentralising in the NSW Public Service," *Journal of Industrial Relations*, 37(2), pp. 203-217.

Purcell, J. (1994) "Human Resources Management: Implications for Teaching, Theory, Research and Practice in Industrial Relations," in Niland, J., Lansbury, R. and Verevis, C. (eds.), *The Future of Industrial Relations*, Sage Publications, pp. 203-218.

Regini, M. (1994) "Human Resource Management and Industrial Relations in European Companies," in Niland, J., Lansbury, R. and Verevis, C. (eds.), *The Future of Industrial Relations*, Sage Publications, pp. 256-269.

Shaw, J.W. (1992) "A New Path to Conflict," *Workplace*, Summer.

Storey, J. (1994) "The Take-up of Human Resource Management by Mainstream Companies: Key Lessons from Research," in Niland, J., Lansbury, R. and Verevis, C. (eds.), *The Future of Industrial Relations*, Sage Publications, pp. 270-292.

Streeck, W. (1991) "The Federal Public of Germany," in Niland, J. and Clarke, O. (eds.), *Agenda for Change: An International*

Analysis of Industrial Relations in Transition, Allen & Unwin, pp. 3-89.

Wever, K. (1994) "On the Future of Trade Unionism in the United States," in Niland, J., Lansbury, R. and Verevis, C. (eds.), *The Future of Industrial Relations* (pp. 185-200), Sage Publications.

Wright, D. (1990) "Playing into the Hands of the Madmen of the Extreme Left," in Easson, M. and Shaw, J. (eds.), *Transforming Industrial Relations*, Pluto Press, pp. 83-87.

Challenges and Opportunities Facing ILERA and Our Field[1]

Thomas A. Kochan

04

One of the greatest honors of my professional career was to serve as president of the International Industrial Relations Association (IIRA), the predecessor organization of our International Labour and Employment Relations (ILERA). It is indeed an equivalent honor to join my distinguished fellow past-presidents in reflecting on the legacy of our Association and to explore how we might advance our field of study in the years ahead.

Indeed, this message is equally relevant to leaders across the globe. It is time to address the deep divisions within and between many of our societies that separate those who are benefiting and those bearing the costs of globalization and changing technologies, those who scapegoat immigrants and those who seek sanctuary from war, persecution, and better lives for their families, and those who believe in equality of opportunity and shared prosperity versus those who are blind or indifferent to inequality. Meeting these challenges requires a renewed commitment to the values and tools on which our field of study, policy, and practice are based. In that spirit I ask that we all rededicate our efforts to working toward these shared goals and values, in this region and across the globe.

Building on ILERA's Legacy

ILERA, indeed the field of industrial relations which ILERA seeks to advance, has a long and distinguished legacy of standing for these values (see Kaufman, 2004 for a thorough review of our field and the history of ILERA). In the mid-nineteenth century Marx was among the first to declare that labour is more than a commodity because physical work could not be separated from human agency and free will. Therefore labour needed to be studied and governed by forces beyond those of the market. His view of course was that labour would only reach its ultimate value when it wrested control of the means of production from capitalists. Later in the same nineteenth century the Webbs modified Marx's views. They agreed labour is more than a commodity but saw workers and their employers embedded in a community; one that would observe an incremental evolution toward democratic socialism in which community values and interests would dominate in labour management relationships and outcomes. In the US John R. Commons and his students and intergenerational followers developed the Wisconsin School of industrial relations by suggesting the conflicts of interest between workers and employers were both enduring and required periodic, but also partial, negotiations and adjustment. Labour and management also shared some common interests and the task of the field of industrial relations was and is to find ways of promoting efficient and equitable solutions to employment problems while respecting and promoting workers' right to have a voice in shaping these conditions.

I repeat these core values, norms, and principles of our field here not because they are either new points, but to remind us of our heritage as we celebrate 50 years of ILERA and look to the future. As the philosopher Santayana warned: those who fail to learn from their past are likely to repeat it. We cannot afford to fall into this trap for the world of work is changing around us in perhaps fundamental ways that will require careful rethinking of some of our basic theoretical propositions and certainly, as our President Dong-One Kim has noted, will continue to challenge us to adapt our empirical research to address the challenges of our time.

This is where I want to focus these remarks: how we can update and advance theory, and research to address what is posed by our Congress hosts, "the challenging question of how to redraw employment relations in order to achieve employment for a sustainable society."

Workers: Who are We?

A good place to start is to consider the workforce as we find it today and to ask, can we continue to assume everyone views work as the central source of their identity? Where does work fit into the constellation of factors that structure our identities and influences our interests, values, and actions as individuals and collective groups at work and in social and political affairs? Since Marx we have assumed that one's role in the division of labour served as the defining factor in shaping one's identity. While competing sources of identity based on gender, family position and ties, tribal or ethnic membership, or other social factors were always present, one's status as a member of the working class or as an agent of those who controlled the means of production and the conditions of labour could be assumed to be the dominant force guiding individual and collective behaviors in employment relationships. Today, given the diversity in the workforce found in and across individual workplaces and societies, this has to be taken as an empirical question (Piore and Safford, 2006). The tensions arising out of cross-border and rural to urban migration, the persistence of racial and ethnic conflicts, the growing awareness and prevalence of sexual harassment, segregation, and discrimination, and the growing recognition of the interdependence of work and family roles and responsibilities all caution us to consider how these factors shape our identities at work and influence how work and employment relationships will evolve in the future. The papers presented in Track 4 remind us that if left unattended these tensions often simmer under the surface until a triggering event generates explosive conflicts that lack effective channels for resolution. When reinforced and sustained over long periods of time by cultural or institutional barriers to mobility and opportunity, inequality and injustice are passed from generation to generation. Unfortunately, as noted in the papers presented in Track 5 on employment relations in emerging economies, the pace of progress in narrowing or closing these regional, gender, and ethnic/racial divisions has slowed in recent years and these tensions are likely to escalate in the future if left unattended. But the research of the young and energetic mix of researchers working on these topics here at the Congress give us reason for optimism. Let us hope that as their work progresses, their findings help reinvigorate and accelerate the pace of progress on the ground.

From Labour-market Dualism to Fissurization of Employment

Equally important sources of diversity in employment relationships are arising out of the phenomenon now known as the fissurization of organizations and employment relationships (Weil, 2014). Moreover, the blurring of the lines separating workers and managers and the growing distance separating many workers from those who have controlling power over their terms and conditions of employment call into question the standard assumptions of a bilateral employment relations model (Barbash, 1964) upon which most of our legacy policies and institutions are based (Riordan and Kowalski, 2018).

This has profound implications for how workers might aggregate their interests at work, or if they even value efforts to mobilize around collective interests derived from their place in the division of labour. For example, today we observe the rise of women in the "Me Too" movement protesting and seeking changes in practices, power relationships, and norms of behavior to eliminate harassment, bullying, and implicit or explicit practices that subjugate women at work. This has produced coalitions that cross class, work roles, and socio-economic status. Similarly, contract workers and independent contractors often have to navigate through multiple labour-market intermediaries in the hiring process and then face questions about which organization if any is responsible for assuring their basic labour standards are met (Rho, 2018). In these settings it is difficult to simply classify parties into standard labour and management roles and identities and it is increasingly difficult to enforce worker rights or build sustainable representative organizations and structures. The discussions taking place at this Congress in Track 3 on "Labour Market Dualism and Institutional Responses" recognize these complexities and produced robust debates and suggested future studies for testing the centrality of work as a source of identity and mobilization versus these other factors. A central question that future research will need to address is whether or how these different sources of identity can be activated and mobilized to support expression and resolution of different interests in ways that improve workplace outcomes (efficiency, equity, and voice) (Budd, 2004). This is the key challenge to both human resource policies and to other institutions and practices governing employment relationships.

The Future of Work

There is an even more radical argument about work promoted by those who see technology eliminating work as we know it for large numbers of people: should we promote guaranteed basic income policies in lieu of expecting everyone to work for a living? Here I believe our interdisciplinary roots give us a concrete hypothesis to challenge this view. Work serves more than instrumental economic functions. Work is also a moral force and provides psychological and social value that would erode the human spirit if replaced by some economic stipend. While all work should provide a living wage and there are income security provisions that are needed to put a floor on personal and family incomes, total replacement of work with an economic endowment is neither economically feasible nor desirable. Research that helps position the role of work in society in the age of advancing digital technologies will be critical to testing this point of view.

There is no question that the most prominent debates over the future of work now relate to the effects of the "Fourth Industrial Revolution" and corresponding advancing digital technologies on employment. Here our field has an important role to play in shifting debates from sterile and highly uncertain predictions about the number of jobs technology will displace or destroy relative to the number it will create. Instead we need to be asking how human actions can influence and shape the future of technology and work in ways that augment and complement work, allow more workers to share in the benefits of advancing technologies and contribute to equality of opportunity, social inclusion and shared prosperity. Indeed I borrow these words from the charge of our MIT Provost to a newly established MIT-wide Task Force on Work of the Future (MIT, 2018). The Provost's charge embodies the best values and traditions of our field: We reject the notion that technological evolution must follow a deterministic path unfettered by any human interventions. Instead, from Marx, to Commons, to today we believe that markets and technologies are subject to human "volitions" as long as we develop through empirical research ways of working in tandem with market and technological forces to shape workplace outcomes.

This is perhaps one of the biggest intellectual challenges facing our field today. The key question is: What changes in practices are needed to influence the future paths of technological advance in constructive ways? I offer one overriding hypothesis that I hope will be the subject of future research: *Integrating the design of technology and the design of work systems and including workers right from the start of this process will produce more efficient and equitable outcomes than the more traditional sequential process in which technology design decisions and choices are made first and issues about how to restructure work and re-skill the workforce are made sequentially and often separately from the design process* (Kochan and Dyer, 2017). Creating opportunities to test this broad hypothesis will require significant organizational and institutional change. Some settings, particularly where labour is viewed and treated as a valued and powerful social partner as in Germany and other Scandinavian countries may be further ahead in this process than countries that have smaller and weaker labour movements and social norms valuing social partnerships. We need to learn from the "natural" variations in institutional arrangements but also to foster experiments that test this hypothesis in settings that are not likely to observe an integrated technology and work system strategies on their own.

Globalization

In his classic essay on the evolution of shoemakers from 1648 to the middle of the nineteenth century (Commons, reprinted, 1985) John R. Commons offered one of our field's most powerful and enduring hypotheses: *If labour-market institutions fail to adapt in ways that match changing product and labour-market conditions, working conditions will be put in competition and decline in quality.* He did not summarize his essay in exactly these words but his careful historical review of the expansion of the product and labour markets for shoemaking as transportation, communications, and technology advanced demonstrated the power of this prediction. That prediction is playing out in modern times in the face of the globalization of markets while most of our labour-market institutions and policies remain national in scope. Our colleague Manfred Weiss noted in his chapter (in this volume) the limited power and impact of the ILO Conventions and enforcement mechanisms for promoting global labour standards. In the absence of global legal regulations, "soft laws" in the form of corporate codes of conduct, and a growing variety of private institutions for improving labour standards in global supply chains have grown up. These have been controversial and subject to a rapidly expanding body of empirical research. To date, this work might be summarized in four statements. First, codes of conduct developed and enforced by multinational corporations have helped upgrade labour standards in global supply chains but reach a threshold level of enforcement that appears to peak at around 60% compliance rates. A study by Distelhorst and McGahan (2018) documents this with data from a large sample of exporters of different products. Their numbers mirror earlier estimates provided by Richard Locke and his associates (Locke, 2013). Thus, corporate codes, if enforced effectively, are steps in the right direction but not sufficient. Second, the same "two equilibria" phenomenon that will be discussed more fully below about "high road" and "low road" strategies found in firms in the same industries in advanced industrial economies appears to exist and have the same effects in global supply chains. Firms that focus on competitive strategies that produce high quality and reliability as opposed to those focusing solely on minimizing costs rely on a bundle of positive workplace practices that improve labour conditions (Distelhorst and McGahan, 2018; Locke, 2013). Third, it is possible but still very difficult to create and sustain multilateral institutional arrangements that promote improved labour standards such as the Accord on Fire and Safety in Bangladesh (Donaghey and Reinecke, 2018). Fourth, all of the above are complementary components in a larger system of policies, institutions, and firm-level practices that need to fit together to create a sustainable pattern of labour standards in global supply chains. The range of complements include firm-level strategies and practices and monitoring systems; independent worker institutions within factories and companies; host governments with strong rule of law regimes on labour and commerce, and perhaps most of all positive interactions among and across the agents of these different contributors to improving labour standards and conditions in globalized operations.

I am pleased to see the good work underway on these topics as illustrated by the papers presented in Track 5 of this Congress. John R. Commons would be proud of this work and would urge it on in ways that help close the gap between lagging nationally bound institutional arrangements and the expanded global market. The reality is this work is still in its very early stages and powerful economic forces militate against sustainable progress. Perhaps it will take more public support, not just public outcries in response to tragic events like the Rana Plaza factory collapse in Bangladesh, but continued pressure from consumers allied with labour organizations to produce sustained progress. Building these alliances and testing for their effects may be one emerging frontier for research on these topics. So too are pro-active efforts of the ILO and other groups to design random controlled experiments to test the effects of different workplace institutions such as safety and health committees on workplace outcomes. Once again, Commons would approve; he was a consummate institutional innovator and builder, including helping to build the first tripartite industrial safety commission in the state of Wisconsin in the early years of the twentieth century.

Worker Voice, Social Dialogue, and Bargaining Power

No issue strikes closer to the heart of industrial relations as a field of study than the decline in union membership experienced in the majority (but not all) advanced economies and the failure of unions to play a major role in many of the more newly industrializing economies (Ibsen and Tapia, 2017). While, as I will note below, it is inaccurate (and certainly unwise) to equate the field of industrial relations or work and employment relations, as we currently call it, with the study of union-management relations, a good deal of empirical research has focused on this topic over many years. This is not surprising given a normative principle on which our field stands that places an important value on worker voice and freedom of association. So the challenge of both understanding the cause of union decline and options for rebuilding worker voice, collective representation, and bargaining power will continue to play a critical role in determining the status of our field. The evidence is clear: the decline in unions and worker representation has led and will continue to lead to a decline in wages and working conditions for large segments of the workforce. In the US, estimates suggest that 20% to 30% of the growth in wage inequality since 1980 is attributable to union decline (Western and Rosenfeld, 2011; Kochan and Riordan, 2016). Others have produced similar estimates for OECD countries (OECD, 2015).

I would offer a rather controversial hypothesis for the future, namely, rebuilding unions in the mirror image of the features that provided them with significant bargaining power in the twentieth century will not be successful. Like all other social and economic institutions, new models of worker voice and representation will be needed that better match the needs and interests of the modern economy and workforce. The search for what these models might entail is a key challenge facing our field and one that has captured and will continue to capture a great deal of innovation and experimentation and therefore provide ample opportunities for research. This is happening all around the world, including here in Korea. The same is true in the US where a wide variety of labour-led coalitions and independent worker advocates are incubating new approaches using various forms of social media, artificial intelligence and machine learning, labour-market and job-matching platforms.

Rethinking Management Roles and Norms

Our field was built on two basic premises regarding employers: (1) the employer responsible for establishing and enforcing basic labour standards could be clearly identified, and (2) employers were expected to meet basic norms of fairness and equity in balancing the interests of investors and owners with the interests of workers and others that contributed to the success of the enterprise. Indeed, the personnel management and later human resource management (HRM) profession grew in size and influence as it became more proficient at managing these responsibilities (Cappelli and Kochan, 1984; Jacoby, 1985; Kaufman, 2004). As the papers in Track 2 of the Congress noted, the fissurization of employing organizations and the growth of what some term financialization of private sector firms calls both premises into question today and has considerably weakened the ability of HRM professionals to carry out these responsibilities. This of course varies across nation states; firms in so-called liberal market economies have allowed these trends to grow and dominate economic affairs more than coordinated market economies. But the trends are similar in direction if not in magnitude across the globe. Building a more broadly and equally shared prosperity will require changes in managerial norms, responsibilities, and the institutions and policies that shape managerial behavior. HRM is now a distributed rather than a centralized responsibility. While this poses enormous intellectual and practical challenges to our field it is only beginning to gain significant recognition in HRM research and to date appears to have produced very little change in HRM practice. Judging from the papers presented at this Congress, however, ILERA researchers are at the forefront of research on this topic.

The broader analysis of managerial norms and behavior outside of the HRM function in recent decades has generated a theoretical argument focused at the level of the individual firm: managers in firms make strategic choices over how to compete and these choices have predictable consequences on employment outcomes. So-called high-road strategies (Kochan and Dyer, 2017; Osterman, 2018), i.e. those that invest in worker training, empower workers to contribute to continuous improvements, accept and support worker voice and social partnerships, and promote high levels of innovation and customer service can both produce high levels of economic performance and support good employment outcomes (Appelbaum, Gittell and Leana, 2011). Those that follow low-road strategies aimed at minimizing costs and controlling workers and suppressing independent worker representation may also produce high levels of economic performance but are destined to also produce poor employment outcomes. The vast literature on high-low road firms and high performance work systems may therefore lead some to expect broader diffusion of these high-road/high-performance work system firms. Yet diffusion varies considerably and, if left on a firm-by-firm basis, has been and is likely to remain partial at best. Indeed, a classic market failure may be at work that limits broad-based diffusion if left to the discretion of individual firms or managerial decision makers. If one firm seeks to shift from a low- to a high-road strategy while its other low-road competitors do not, the former may lose competitive ground in the short run. Given this expectation, firms will remain stuck in the low equilibrium position.

Overcoming this type of classic market failure requires coordinated actions at a level above the individual firm through employer associations, unions or other labour-market institutions, or government policies that raise the floor on labour standards to reduce space for low-road firms and/or reward high-road firms in some way; an issue taken up in the final section below.

Toward a New Social Contract

I often draw on the metaphor of a "social contract at work," i.e. the mutual expectations and obligations that workers, employers, and their communities and societies have for work and employment relationships (Kochan, 2000) to describe the overarching challenge of our time. The divisions in societies, the growth in income inequality and the persistent gap between productivity and wage growth are visible indicators of the need for a new social contract. The central argument running through my research and teaching about how to build a new social contract is that *overcoming these divisions and building a more inclusive economy cannot be achieved without the engagement of multiple stakeholders.* Historically our field has focused on three parties - employers, workers and their organizations, and government as the primary actors in employment relations (Dunlop, 1958). Given the importance of knowledge in modern economies I would add educational institutions as a fourth actor. This is especially important in a world of continuously evolving new technologies. Lifelong learning is now an imperative for building and maintaining workforce skills.

The challenge lies in engaging these four parties and perhaps other groups in coordinated efforts needed to build a new social contract. In Europe there is a long tradition of the "social partners" engaging in dialogue on major social and economic problems at various levels of society. From time to time countries such as Korea, Australia, and to a lesser extent Great Britain have likewise put structures in place to support negotiations over one or more national economic or employment policies. The US has less of this tradition outside of special wartime circumstances. Yet our field specializes in engaging groups with different interests in dialogue, negotiations, and problem solving. I can think of no bigger challenge or responsibility before us at this juncture in history than to find ways to foster constructive dialogue across these groups in search of policies that heal our deep divisions and build a more productive and equitable future. Our success or failure to do so may indeed be the legacy by which our generation of labour and employment relations professionals leaves to future generations.

Shaping the Future of Work

I hope these remarks make it clear that I believe we have a lot to offer and a lot to do if we are to improve the world of work for generations to come. In taking up the challenge our Congress hosts posed it is important to keep in mind what the founders of our field argued: neither markets nor technologies are deterministic. They are shaped by the ideas, interests, motivations, and innovative actions of humans. Moreover, the power of human creativity and action is often felt most strongly when channeled in collective efforts involving respectful and constructive dialogue and negotiations among people or groups with different perspectives and interests. Our profession, indeed our societies, may have lost some momentum in recent years because we have not put our ideas and tools to their maximum uses. Let's hope the creative energy that went into planning this Congress and that is evident in the papers and discussions presented in this chapter signal a renewed commitment to applying our core values, theories, and ideas in new ways. This, indeed, will bode well for the future of our field of study and for our world.

Note

1 Paper prepared for presentation for the session commemorating the 50th Anniversary of the International Labour and Employment Relations (ILERA) at the 18th World Congress of ILERA, Seoul, South Korea, July 25, 2018.

References

Appelbaum, E., Hoffer Gittell, J. and Leana, C. (2011)

High-performance Work Practices and Sustainable Economic Growth. Washington, D.C., Center for Economic and Policy Research.

Barbash, J. (1964) "The Elements of Industrial Relations," *Br. J. Ind. Relations*, 10(2), pp. 66-78.

Budd, J.W. (2004) *Employment with a Human Face: Balancing Efficiency, Equity, and Voice*, Cornell University Press.

Cappelli, P. and Kochan, T.A. (1984) "The Transformation of the Industrial Relations and Personnel Function," in Osterman, P. (ed.), *Internal Labour Markets,* The MIT Press.

Commons, J.R. (1980) "American Shoemakers: 1648-1895," in Rowan, R. (ed.), *Readings in Labour Economics and Labour Relations* (4th edition), Richard D. Irwin.

Distelhorst, G. and McGahan, A. (2018) *Internal Stakeholders and Socially Irresponsible Employment:* Evidence from Exporters in Emerging Markets, Working paper.

Donaghey, J. and Reinecke, J. (2018) "When Industrial Democracy Meets Corporate Social Responsibility - A Comparison of the Bangladesh Accord and Alliance as Responses to the Rana Plaza Disaster," *Br. J. Ind. Relations*, 56(1), pp. 14-42.

Dunlop, J.T. (1958) *Industrial Relations Systems*, Harvard Business School Press.

Ibsen, C.L. and Tapia, M. (2017) "Trade Union Revitalisation: Where Are We Now? Where to Next?" *J. Ind. Relations*, 59(2), pp. 170-191.

Jacoby, S. (1985) *Employing Bureaucracies*, Columbia University Press.

Kaufman, B.E. (2004) *The Global Evolution of Industrial Relations*, International Industrial Relations Association.

Kochan, T.A. (2000) "Building a New Social Contract at Work: A Call to Action," *Perspect.* Work 4(1), pp. 3-12.

Kochan, T.A. and Dyer, L. (2017) *Shaping the Future of Work: A Handbook for Action and a New Social Contract*, MIT Press.

Kochan, T.A. and Riordan, C.A. (2016) "Employment Relations and Growing Income Inequality: Causes and Potential Options for Its Reversal," *J. Ind. Relations*, 58(3), pp. 419-440.

Locke, R.M. (2013) *The Promise and Limits of Private Power: Promoting Labour Standards in a Global Economy*, Cambridge University Press.

Massachusetts Institute of Technology (MIT). (2018) *MIT Task Force on the Work of the Future*. https://workofthefuture.mit.edu/.

OECD. (2015) *In It Together: Why Less Inequality Benefits All*, OECD Publishing.

Osterman, P. (2018) "In Search of the High Road: Meaning and Evidence," *ILR Rev.* 71(1), pp. 3-34.

Piore, M.J. and Safford, S. (2006) "Changing Regimes of Workplace Governance, Shifting Axes of Social Mobilization and the Challenge to Industrial Relations Theory," *Ind. Relat. (Berkeley)*, 45(3), pp. 299-326.

Rho, H.J. (2018) Rise of *Multicentric Employment Relationships: What Are the Implications for HR and ER Theory?* Working paper.

Riordan, C.A. and Kowalski, A.M. (2018) *The Social Formation of Conflict and the Challenges it Poses to Industrial Relations Theory*. Working paper.

Weil, D. (2014) *The Fissured Workplace: Why Work Became So Bad for So Many and What Can Be Done to Improve It*, Harvard University Press.

Western, B. and Rosenfeld, J. (2011) "Unions, Norms, and the Rise in U.S. Wage Inequality," *Am. Sociol. Rev.*, 76(4), pp. 513-537.

Employment for a Sustainable Society: What is to be Done?

Tiziano Treu

05

Reframing Our Field of Study

Our field of study and its object, labour and employment relations, have always been changing. Even the name of our association had changed in 2007, not a common event in the area of the social sciences. The history of the association and this very anniversary provide vast evidence of these changes. In the past, like today, the impact of social and economic transformations has questioned our assumptions and forced us to adapt many aspects of our theories and policy proposals.

What is specific to our times is the speed of change and the depth of the challenges which the great transformations of the world scenario present not only to labour regulations but to the existing social and economic systems.

The challenges are so fundamental that quite a few experts in our field, not to speak of managers and politicians, envisage the decline of labour regulations.[1] A recent analysis based on quantitative analysis of Industrial Relations change has argued that the trajectories of most (advanced) countries indicate a clear trend toward a universal neoliberal transformation of industrial relations and in general of the capitalistic systems, which would contradict the traditional interpretative model of the varieties of capitalism.

In this perspective, which is indeed quite controversial, the decline of traditional industrial relations based on collective agreements as a major source of labour regulations might be substituted by human resource management and other forms of individual relations. A similar possibility would have a direct impact also on the study of labour relations. A decline in legal and collective regulations, challenged by market force and substituted by managerial decisions, would cause a parallel reduction or irrelevance of our discipline.[2]

However it is a fact that the forms of work and of employment relations built in the past century are threatened by the structural factors that alter most aspects of the economy and of the social life, namely globalization and technological innovations. Both factors are not new, but their influence has been growing in the last years at an unprecedented pace.

Even so there is evidence, and I will mention some, that the impact of these factors is not predetermined, but is influenced by the existing institutions and by the political decisions adopted in different times and in the various countries. Here is the space for the initiative of the actors, public and private, which operate in the spheres of the social, economic and political life.

There is also a great opportunity for our studies. With their tradition of critical thinking and experience of interdisciplinary research they may face the difficult challenges of the world of work more appropriately than other disciplines characterized by a less critical and more prescriptive approach to the analysis and management of employment relations.

The challenges to our discipline are so fundamental that no minor adaptation of the traditional policies is sufficient to restore the role of labour law and of industrial relations as effective instruments of social justice and of economic progress. A vast amount of common effort is needed for understanding the underlying factors of these challenges.

We need also to stress the importance of a comparative approach. Even though the object of our discipline has been built for a century on a national basis, now it is facing an increased interdependence not only among enterprises and financial institutions, but also between the entire legal and social systems of the various countries.

Comparative analysis - which is different from simple description of the various national systems - is not easy for scholars and for policy makers who have for decades focused on domestic issues, relying on the specificity of their own solutions. Here too, our associations, and this meeting, provide good examples of innovative comparative research in many areas of labour and industrial relations.[3]

The complexity of these issues and the richness of the experience accumulated over the years does not allow for easy solutions and shortcuts. Broad analysis of the general economic and social trends may be insufficient or misleading. More detailed in-depth analysis is necessary to understand the multifaceted reality of employment and of labour regulations and to detect the reactions of the various social and legal systems to the present challenges.[4] Even minute solutions may be important for daily life. Specific micro analysis is important in a period of rapid and uncertain transitions where partial innovations in some areas may be relevant to indicate future evolutions of each system.

European Experiences: A Testing Ground

Given the limit of this presentation and of my knowledge, I will concentrate on some traits of labour regulations adopted in Europe, both by the Union and by member states. These European regulations may be a significant testing ground for detecting the reactions of labour law and industrial relations to the transformations of the world of work. The analysis of these reactions may also offer some arguments to test the opinions mentioned above which envisage an inevitable decline of Industrial Relations.

The various European states have different historical traditions and maintain quite a few differences in labour regulations, particularly so if we consider the Eastern countries, which the European Union has been recently enlarged. But being members of the European Union has intensified the relations among the various countries and the exchange of practices also in labour matters. Moreover the Union, as such, has contributed to the spread of common practices and rules in the field of employment and industrial relations, which have built a common social dimension, usually referred to as the "social model."[5]

Relative to most other areas of the world this "model" is characterized by high standards in the major aspects of labour regulations: guarantees of collective and individual social rights, statutory legal and collective regulations of working conditions; social security and welfare institutions which protect workers from the risks of work and respond to the essential needs of life; extensive practices of collective bargaining; and of worker participation.

The European Charter of Fundamental Rights has solemnly confirmed the commitment of the Community and of its member states to observe and implement the basic social standards which are internationally recognized and which are a necessary component of "decent work."[6]

The European model represents a quite unique approach to supranational labour regulations, legally more stringent than other forms, bilateral treaties and the like. This peculiar approach allows for multi-level regulatory interventions, national and European, on most labour problems.[7]

In spite of these achievements the established system of social rights and policies has not fully protected the European workers and citizens from the damages of the recent economic crisis. And it does not exempt our countries from facing new risks and challenges of the future. Indeed these challenges are quite similar to those common to the rest of the world, which threaten the stability of traditional labour regulations and policies.

In recent years the most dramatic challenge has come from the economic crisis which has hit Europe with an even greater impact than for non-European countries, and has seriously deteriorated the social and economic conditions of its citizens. The measures implemented by the EU member states in order to react to this crisis have affected all major public policies in the field of labour and social matters. The results of these measures have been uneven and quite variable among the different member states. Indeed these differences seem to be on the increase and indicate a divergence, even a polarization, among the various regions of Europe, with marked divides North-South and East-West. This trend is contrary to the objective pursued by the Union to promote a gradual convergence among the national systems, if not a harmonization of their main features.[8]

The need to revise the traditional social policies has not ceased after the crisis, because the factors which challenge the traditional way of intervening in employment and industrial relations issues have proved to persist even with the economic recovery, so confirming their structural character.

Changing Protective Labour Legislation: Simplifications and Flexibility

In this chapter I will analyze some changes in European labour regulations and policies which appear to be particularly significant in showing the capacity of our systems to respond and to adapt to the transformation of the world of work and where the European experience may be useful for comparative analysis.

I am aware that labour law and public institutions acting in the area of employment, Industrial Relations and welfare are a limited part of the economic and social order. Consequently, they have a partial impact on the functioning of our systems. But throughout our history state policies have always been important, if not decisive, in shaping employment relations, and in general, to regulate the power relations between labour and capital. My assumption is that their capacity to respond to the new challenges is still important for the future of work. The role of national states, although limited by globalization, remains essential in regulating major social issues, and indeed also in influencing the trend and impact of globalization.[9]

The complexity of present changes, which involve different policies, different actors and different levels of governance and regulations, can be fully understood only with in-depth comparative and multidisciplinary research. Indeed the elements and results now acquired are in my view far from being uniform and conclusive.

The EU countries have followed different strategies to fight the crisis and then to face the new-world scenario depending on their social and political conditions. A common remark by comparatists is that the search for effective innovative policies is still open and proceeds with more uncertainties than with defined targets.[10] Most issues receive controversial or contradictory opinions and solutions. A first controversial area has to do with the scope and the content of protective labour legislation. In fact the intensity and rigidity of labour legislations of most European countries have been accused of producing negative effects on economic efficiency and dynamism, even though the evidence is controversial and far from conclusive.[11]

One reaction of many national legislators has been to try to simplify labour regulations and make them more selective and tailored to the different needs and positions of the employees, including those working with non-standard contracts. A common trend was to implement a new regulatory approach, more simplified and better finalized, with the declared aim of mitigating the dualism of the labour markets.[12]

Another common trend has been to respond to the need of the enterprises to adapt to the new competitive and technological scenario, by introducing and regulating various forms of flexibility. Numerical and external flexibility has been increased in two main directions: by reducing the sanctions for unjust dismissals and consequently their cost, by recognizing flexible types of employment contracts that differ from the typical employment contract for an indefinite period. The extent of these changes and their impact on worker stability has been different according to the measures adopted by the various states in order to regulate the various forms of flexibility.

Sheer deregulation has not been the rule; most often the law has reduced some aspects of legal rigidity while maintaining basic principles and protections of the workers: e.g. the principle of just cause for the justification of dismissals. An important variable has been the capacity of the unions to control the use of flexibility by the employers. The power of the unions has been affected to a different degree according to the economic and political context of the various states. In most countries it has been reduced as shown by the main relevant indicators: decreasing union density and reduced rate of conflict, shrinking collective bargaining coverage and decentralization of bargaining structure.[13] But still, major differences persist among countries. The rate of unionization varies from a maximum of 67-70%

of the Northern Countries to a low of 7.7% (France); and the dispersion around the average rate has been growing.[14] This dispersion supports a possible trend toward divergence, or even polarization, more than toward convergence.[15]

In some countries (Germany, Belgium and also Italy) the power of the unions remains considerable not only at the national level but also, and some time even more so, at the company level where workers' representatives of various kinds maintain well-defined rights of participation and control.

The European Policy of Flexicurity: Different National Implementations

The risk of the increased flexibility and its impact on worker stability have been denounced by the unions of many countries and by international organizations like the International Labour Organization (ILO) which have stressed the need to regulate the use of flexibility in order to make it compatible with decent work.[16]

A major policy suggested by the EU in a specific set of guidelines on "flexicurity," which may be interesting for other systems,[17] has been intended to compensate for the negative effects of flexibility by introducing or reinforcing various measures aimed at protecting and assisting all displaced workers. The measures consist not only in monetary subsidies to these workers but in active policies (placement services, training and re-training), intended to facilitate their re-entry into the labour market. The effectiveness of these measures to keep the balance between flexibility and security has been uneven. It has been better maintained in some countries (central and Northern Europe) and are well equipped with active labour policies and with strong welfare systems. Lacking these conditions, the balance has been precarious and the measures aimed at workers security have not always protected them from the risks of unemployment.[18]

The economic crisis of the last decade has increased the difficulty in keeping this balance, particularly to protect and assist the displaced workers for the time necessary for their reinstatement. For this reason the European Parliament has proposed a reframing of the policy of flexicurity.[19]

Some European countries have introduced or reinforced measures aimed at preventing, as much as possible, the dismissals of employees of firms that are hit by economic crisis or are involved in restructuring processes.[20] A major provision has been to guarantee the payment of an indemnity, up to 60-60% of the salary by social security institutions to the employees suspended by their employers for those reasons. This financed suspension, which in some cases could last up to 3-4 years, has allowed the employers to pass the bad times or to restructure their firms without mass dismissals.

Another measure adopted has been to grant to employers a wide discretion to introduce flexible working time and to change employees' job assignments. This increased flexibility has been often accompanied by the duty, fixed by law or by collective agreements, to retrain the employees for the new posts.[21]

This form of functional flexibility, particularly when introduced in agreement with worker representatives, has proved useful in reducing the recourse to alternative measures of external flexibility such as outsourcing and use of temporary fixed-term contracts. In a few cases it has also contributed to improve both the working conditions and productivity. These practices are being analyzed by a research group organized by the International Society for Labour and Social Security Law (ISLSSL).

A redefinition of scope and contents is necessary not only for the institutions dealing with labour problems but also for those present in the area of social security and welfare.[22] A more active set of policies is needed both to reduce the increasing costs of social benefits and to mobilize the capacities of users, in order to promote their personal development and not simply to assist them in case of need.

An opportunity to be caught is to exploit the potentials of individuals, and even of individualism, by supporting personal trajectories in the various life cycles and by investing in the different personal qualities of people to shape their "capabilities." In this perspective welfare measures can be seen as more than just a cost, it is a social investment,[23] and can prove to be not only compatible with, but functional to sustainable growth and competitiveness.

This new approach to welfare measures may facilitate their extension beyond the traditional coverage of core employees to non-standard workers and to the growing number of migrant workers which have been, so far, excluded from protection and mostly ignored.

A major challenge to the welfare systems, even of the rich countries, is posed by the growth of inequalities and poverty among the various sectors of the population, including many workers. Specific measures of income support and of personal assistance for poor workers and families have been introduced in many European countries, combined with targeted labour and training policies aimed at activating the beneficiaries. Proposals of extending assistance measures or provisions of "basic income" have been deemed inacceptable for their costs but also because they tend to obscure the value of work and the importance of employment policies.

The Impact of the Digital Revolution on the Future of Work

These measures, like most employment practices, must now face the challenges posed by the digital revolution, which is introducing profound transformations both in the organization of work (telework, on demand employment via digital platforms) and in the structure of the enterprises.

Like most innovations, industry 4.0 implies new risks and opportunities: risks for the conditions of work (increasing stress and psychological diseases, deskilling, etc.) but also opportunities for better work-life balance and for improving the autonomy and the personalization of work.[24]

The impact of the digital revolution on the future quantity of jobs is quite controversial. Platform-based work has still limited applications. In Europe it accounts for no more than 1% of employment; but in the US this percentage is already higher.[25]

In any case the various types of digital work have great potential to grow. Already a significant number of jobs have been made redundant by the spreading of ICT, particularly in sectors like banking and insurance once considered to be the home of stability. But whatever the possible impact of these technologies, the key challenge for us, as T. Kochan, in this book, rightly points out, is to find policies capable of influencing the future of technologies in constructive ways. These policies are complex and not yet well defined.

It is worth mentioning that the digital threat has reopened, at least in Europe, the debate not only on work-time flexibility but also on the reduction of working time.[26] Part-time working (not always voluntary) is increasing and becoming a common way of redistributing work, often within the family. In the Netherlands it accounts for around half of the working population. A recent German collective agreement has recognized the right of all employees to reduce temporarily (for 2 years) their weekly working time to 28 hours (with some wage reduction) and the parallel right to return to the number of hours previously worked (35). In exchange, the employers are allowed greater flexibility in the distribution of weekly working time. This agreement is considered an example of flexibility beneficial to both parties.

Other collective agreements, particularly in the sectors most exposed to the digital revolution, have provided that a certain number of working hours, regularly paid, must be devoted to training and re-training in order to prevent technological obsolescence of employees. This indeed is a requirement common to all sectors of any country, since it is necessary to cope with technological innovations. More time and resources will have to be devoted to education and training of employees, not only at the early stages of their working career and during the apprenticeship, but in the entire course of their life.[27]

Some European countries like Italy, in order to promote this policy, are combining strong fiscal incentives to the introduction of new technologies in the enterprise with parallel incentives to the training of the workers exposed to these technologies. An objective present in the European debate, but worth considering also in other countries, is that all employment contracts should become educational contacts, i.e. should enrich the basic exchange of the contract - work versus wage - with a further element, namely with a certain amount of training.

Adaptation to Changing Working Patterns

Whatever the quantitative evolution of work might be in the near future, certainly most working patterns, including the flexible works adopted so far, will have to change; and equally widespread changes will be necessary for the personal skills required for performing the new jobs. The very concept of working time as traditionally framed is being altered in the digital organization of work. The online connection necessary for the digital employees may blur the distinction between time for work and time for life, with negative implications for personal wellbeing (risk for ill health and danger of self-exploitation).

Rigid legal limitations of working time are unfeasible or easy to be circumvented. New measures, legal and collective, may be necessary. Some suggestions may come from recent European practices. Some collective agreements in Germany and the legislators in France and Italy have introduced the so-called "right to disconnection," i.e. the right of employees to cease to be available online during certain periods of the day and night (taking into account the different time zones where digital workers may operate) and have provided the consequent duty of the employer to disconnect the server.

The digitalization of the work process requires innovations in two other critical areas of labour law and labour policies: health and safety regulation, and protection of employees' privacy.[28] Both represent common challenges to all advanced economies. The need to prevent and remedy not only the physical risks known to the industrial reduction, but other psychological disorders which are already increasing in the information society, has been recognized by some countries that have reframed their legislation on health and safety so to include the new risks.

New Risks for Health and Safety, and for Personal Privacy

The national institutes in charge of work accidents have begun to adapt the requisites and the tariffs for the relevant insurance to the peculiar conditions of remote work.

Moreover, some national legislators (including Italy)[29] have enacted specific regulations to protect workers' privacy, business operations and secrecy. All enterprises are required to implement procedural rules, under the responsibility of plant managers, aimed at preventing any use of digital devices capable of violating employee privacy (violations are severely sanctioned). The use of devices which can control employees activity must be approved by workers representatives and/or by the labour inspectors; moreover the data collected through these devices cannot be ground for disciplinary sanctions against the employees. A controversial issue is how to regulate the use of devices which are necessary for performing the job and at the same time may indirectly control employee activity. The management practices will have to be carefully monitored in order to clarify this issue and possibly to adapt the regulations to the evolution of technological devices.

The conditions of work created by the new forms of business organization, which are often more demanding than in the past, and the new needs and aspirations of present employees have stimulated an increased demand for quality in working life.

Search for a Better Work-Life Balance

In response to this demand many collective agreements signed at the firm level in quite a few European countries have devoted greater attention to controlling the implementation of technological innovations and to preventing their negative effects on working conditions. The impact of these collective regulations has been favored by various forms of workers participation to the process of innovation, which in some countries have been supported by legislation.[30]

A parallel trend of some agreements has been to introduce positive measures not only for improving health and safety but also for promoting a better work-life balance. To this end they have introduced personal and family-friendly working hours, and various kinds of benefits supplementing public welfare aimed at fostering the wellbeing of people at work (care services for children and aged relatives, support for children's education and leisure, medical assistance and pensions more generous that those provided by the state). The number of these agreements has been growing (in Italy they are counted by the thousands) because they have been promoted by fiscal advantages, which exempt most welfare benefits agreed upon with the unions from taxation.[31] A reduced taxation has also been provided on wages linked to various indicators of productivity defined by collective agreements. The rationale, which has been accepted by the unions, is to promote a wage structure less rigid than in the past and more conducive to productivity. Moreover, the same Italian legislation has provided a further fiscal prize when these productivity bonuses and welfare benefits are accompanied with forms of worker participation in the organization of work within the firms, through bilateral committees with employer representatives. This promotional legislation has contributed to the diffusion of worker participation in the enterprise. This kind of participation is quite common in countries like Germany and France and is promoted by a specific European directive (2001/8 and regulation 2157/2001), but was so far resisted in Italy, mainly for ideological reasons.

The Workers of the Gig Economy: Problems of Categorization and of Protection

The information technologies and the digital economy have contributed to multiply the forms of work: a trend which requires new legal and contractual regulations.

The rules adopted in the European countries are variable, but have in common the tendency mentioned above to give more space than in the past to flexibility. Equally common is the recognition that the traditional categorization of employment contracts is not adequate to fully reflect the content of many "atypical" contracts which have emerged in the mobile labour market of today. Even the basic demarcation between subordinate employment and self-employment is becoming less and less clear.[32] The platform-based work is an exemplary case.

European legislators have introduced various measures to regulate the new types of work, most often with the aim of mitigating the fragmentation and the dualism of the labour market. The criteria for identifying subordination have been loosely interpreted by some courts. Quite a few social protections are being extended to atypical contracts. Various mechanisms, a mix of incentives and controls, have been experimented in order to formalize informal work (which is widely present also in developed countries).[33]

A relatively new type of worker has been growing; they are not legally subordinate, but neither are they fully autonomous because they are economically dependent on one or a few principles. The legislators of some countries have created an intermediate category of contracts with various names: quasi-subordinate employees (Italy), employee-like persons (Germany) or workers (UK). To these employees some, but not all, rules of labour law apply: mainly those concerning social security, health and safety, minimum wages and other minimum standards, rights of association and of collective bargaining.

The various forms of digital works present in the gig economy have posed new problems of categorization, because these employees often combine traits typical of both dependent and independent work.[34] These problems have been, so far, mostly handled by the national courts in hundreds of cases, which have received divergent solutions.[35] In quite a few cases, mainly involving Uber drivers or the "riders" of Foodora, the courts have defined them as employees, even when not all traditional indicators of subordination were present. Other courts have considered them independent contractors, or included in the intermediate category mentioned above. Sometimes the judges have recognized the hybrid character of their work in order to grant some, but not all the protections of labour law. The need to bestow some basic protections to these workers has prevailed over the uncertainty of the legal qualification of the contract.

A similar approach has been adopted by the French legislature in 2016 (Act. August 8, 2016, n. 1088, art. 6). While giving a rather general definition of digital workers, this Act provides that they are entitled to some basic rights such as the right to continuous education and training, to protection against work accidents;[36] the right of association, of collective bargaining and of strike. The European Court of Justice has decided that Uber is not a mere platform for the intermediation of work, but an enterprise involved in transport and logistic activities. Consequently, it is obliged to follow the national rules on these activities, not necessarily those concerning labour matters (but the road is open to also consider labour regulations).[37]

The issue is still controversial, particularly because the typology of activities organized in the gig economy is highly differentiated and variable. For example, the criteria applied to Uber drivers does not fit many crowd-workers who perform minute and short tasks through personal access to digital platforms, which do not exercise any kind of interference nor direction of their activities.

The Impact of Change on Labour Unions and Collective Agreements

The changes of the economic context and the diversification of work require a reappraisal not only of employment policies, but also of collective bargaining and industrial relations. How to do it is a controversial issue that has received different solutions by those, governments and social parties, who consider collective bargaining and industrial relations an important instrument of social participation and of employee protection, and not an obstacle to the functioning of the economy.

Collective agreement has been shaped, like statutory law, according to the dominant patterns of standard employment and is mostly based on the experience of industrialized countries. If they are to remain a major source of regulation of employment, they too must revise their objectives and practices so as to respond to the diversification of employment patterns, and on the other hand to the globalization of markets.

Indeed these transformations are affecting the system of industrial relations even more directly than the legal status of the contract of employment, in so far as industrial relations are exposed, often without any protection, to the pressures of the markets, and because the diversification of work affects the very basis of collective action of the workers, more than the initiatives of the employers.

These factors have altered the power relations among the social parties to the detriment of the labour unions and account for the growing difficulties of traditional industrial relations which are visible, even in the strongest systems of central and northern Europe. However, here too, the responses of the various national actors are far from uniform as it is shown by the main indicators, in particular by the variation in union density. Moreover the decline in average union density and the even more pronounced decline of industrial conflict, which has been confined to the public sector, are not fully reflected in the coverage and in the structure of collective bargaining. Here the variations among countries are different from those of union density due to the impact of other factors, in particular of legislation and of public policies concerning industrial relations.

The coverage of national collective agreements has continued to be relatively high in countries where the rate of unionization has been traditionally low, such as France and Spain, and has further declined in recent years. This is due mainly to state legislature that have supported the application of national or multiemployer collective agreements beyond the area of the unions' influence by way of various mechanisms of legal extension of these agreements to all the firms and employees of the various economic sectors.[38] This promotional legislation has not changed, and indeed has been reinforced in some countries like Germany: while in the past the extension could be decided on the condition that the agreement covered the majority of the interested firms and employees, recent legislation has lifted this condition in order to facilitate the extension. It has provided that the extension can be ordered at the request of the bargaining parties following a discretionary evaluation of the public authorities. Moreover minimum wages have been introduced in Germany, one of the few countries of Europe, together with Italy, where they did not exist as a way to sustain the salaries of occasional and precarious types of work, so-called mini jobs, which are much lower than the average.[39]

Even in the countries like Italy where a legal system of extension does not exist, other forms of indirect support of the effects of the agreements are in place. Court decisions and administrative provisions require the respect of the standards fixed by national agreements as a condition to receive various fiscal benefits. The same wage standards are relevant to determine the basis for social security contributions. The role and effectiveness of collective agreements have been indirectly sustained, also by the law which recognizes the right to bargain only belonging to representative unions, in order to oppose the fragmentation and hence the weakening of the bargaining parties. These legal interventions have been important in supporting collective agreements; even though it is doubtful that they may be sufficient to redress the balance of power which is now unfavorable for the unions.

Another form of promotional legislation has been adopted by some countries, and endorsed by an EU directive which grants consultation and participation rights to workers' representatives on major enterprise decisions affecting working conditions. The experience of countries where this participation is widely adopted has shown positive results not only in facilitating employment relations, but also in improving both the welfare of workers and the productivity of firms.

This approach however requires a major change of attitude in the culture and practice of the social parties, particularly of the unions most dedicated to conflict and alien to participation. An institutional support to participative industrial relations comes also in those countries where unions and employers associations have developed, with legal endorsement, a net of bilateral committees and organizations which administer a considerable number of welfare and training instruments. These bilateral institutions have proved resistant to the economic crisis and often the changes of government.

Decentralization of Collective Bargaining Structure

The transformation of work and of the markets have exerted strong pressure to decentralize the structure of collective bargaining, which in quite a few European countries was rather centralized, as reflected in the central position of national sectoral agreements.[40]

Decentralized bargaining, mainly to the company and plant level, has acquired a decisive role in most countries even where the national and multiemployer agreements were traditionally prevalent.

The national legislators have encouraged this process of decentralization on various conditions and with a different impact on the role of national agreements. Some legislation (Spain) have completely altered the traditional hierarchy of the bargaining structure by attributing to company agreements the primary role in regulating most labour issues, including the possibility to fix conditions of work less favorable to employees than those set nationally.

A more nuanced solution has been adopted in France where the law has attributed priority to decentralized agreements in the regulation of some issues not reserved to national agreements, but it has provided the duty of the employers to bargain periodically over most labour matters.[41]

Similar measures have been decided, although less clearly, by Italian law, which has awarded to decentralized agreements, contrary to tradition, the same legal status and effectiveness as the national agreements.[42] Moreover, collective bargaining has been promoted, with the fiscal incentives mentioned above, in specific areas, because some fiscal incentives have been reserved, such as productivity bonuses and welfare benefits, to be bargained with the unions, and not to those unilaterally decided by management. In countries like Germany and Italy the central labour unions have been able to control the process of decentralization,[43] at least in the strong economic sectors and in medium to large firms, and have used the possibility to derogate from the national standards mainly in cases of serious economic crisis in order to prevent mass dismissals and plant closures.

In sum, these trends indicate a marked alteration of the structure of continental collective bargaining. The national agreements are becoming similar to framework contracts[44] setting basic standards and guidelines more than regulating the actual conditions of work. Wages tend to be linked, above the minima, to the performance of workers and to indicators of business productivity and results. Decentralized agreements tend to become firm-specific, i.e. dedicated to solving problems of work organization and to administer the daily life of the workplace, mostly through specialized procedures and bilateral committees. In many advanced companies participatory bargaining is competing with innovative human resource management for the allegiance of the new and old types of employees.[45] For the reasons already explained, public support to collective activities is important even more than in the past. But the future of the industrial relations depends in the first place on the capacity of the labour movement to find new reasons and objectives for a common action.

The growth and influence of the European unions have been built, differently from the trend prevailing in the USA, not only on collective bargaining, but on a vast spectrum of social and political actions, including the participation within the enterprises and in public institutions in charge of labour policies, training and welfare policies. The value of this multiplicity of arenas in the face of the present global transformations, has been confirmed by most European unions, even though their relations with the traditional labour parties has been loosened, and the declining fortunes of labour-friendly governments have often reduced their financial and institutional support to unions' activities.

The decline of membership and the increasingly difficult relationship with the state have persuaded many European unions to experiment innovative forms of recruiting activities similar to those practiced by American unions, in particular toward the new types of employees, skilled and unskilled, which populate the present labour markets. But these practices of union revitalization have met with an uneven degree of success, due to the difficulty in overcoming the obstacles, which contrast collective action and organization.

Forms of collaboration and alliance with other types of social movements have been sought by some unions, but in most cases they have remained at an initial stage due to the difficulty of finding common objectives with the traditional goals and often of the resistance of the unions' leadership. In fact greater attention has been given by the unions of the major countries to service activities of different kinds (social assistance, training services), which have proved useful not only to increase the allegiance of members and the attractiveness of membership, but also to compensate for the reduced amount of member dues and of public resources.

The decentralization process of Industrial Relations has been promoted by employers' associations, but they have not pushed to abolish national and multiemployer bargaining, in this respect, converging with the position of the unions. Workers organizations are committed to safeguarding the social function of national agreements as a guarantee of equality in the basic conditions of work for the employees of the same economic sector. The employers' associations have accepted to maintain this level of bargaining even though reduced in content and made more flexible, in order to respond to the different needs of the firms, because national agreements have proved to be useful to regulate employment contracts of the multitude of small firms, often marginal, which represent the majority in many sectors of the economy. Centralized bargaining has been useful also to exempt these firms from the direct impact of unions and social pressure. At the same time national agreements leave room for the more productive enterprises to regulate differently their employees according to their specific needs.

Global Trade and Fundamental Rights: The Social Clauses in International Treaties

A different challenge to traditional labour regulations comes from the diffusion of work and of the enterprises on a global scale. This challenge is often combined with or intensified by the innovations coming from the new technologies, because these technologies multiply the possibility to expand most activities beyond the national borders. The challenge goes to the roots of our discipline, because our legal systems, particularly those concerning labour relations, have been nationally based and have been supported by national policies and regulations. This has occurred often in accordance with the social parties. These issues are the object of discussion for the research group n. 3 of the ISLSSL.

The unions have recently tried to expand their organization and some activities, including strike action, at the supranational level. But the resources devoted to these activities are still limited and have not brought to the international workers representatives sufficient power to face the influence of multinational enterprises. The need to act in this new scenario and to project, internationally, labour regulations and social policies is widely recognized. But more political and intellectual investments are necessary to change the contents and techniques of national regulations and policies in order to enable them to operate effectively across national borders. The objective of international labour regulations is not only to protect the increasing number of people who work across the borders, but also to defend the national standards of work from unfair competition of the firms operating in foreign countries. Part of the challenge is that the law is called to reconcile the commercial logic of trade with the need to guarantee basic social rights of the workers involved in international trade.

The various national actors, public institutions, employers' associations and labour unions, together with the relevant international organizations, have been trying to respond to this challenge and have adopted different techniques to shape supranational principles and regulations.[46]

The complexity of the issues involved and the variety of the actors of international trade has given rise to a diversification of forms of regulation: directives and recommendations of international organizations (ILO, OECD in the first place); social clauses inserted in international treaties; general systems of preference (GSP); codes of practices of multinational enterprises; transnational collective agreements.

The difference of these sources and of the matters affected has brought about an extreme variety of contents and techniques of regulation, as well as different systems of implementation. The whole spectrum of regulatory systems developed in past national and international experiences has found here a fertile ground of application.

The European Union and its member states have attempted to promote the international respect of some basic labour standards through the insertion of social clauses in multinational trade agreements and with other instruments, such as the GSP.[47]

A similar objective is pursued by multilateral agreements signed in different areas of the world (the Trans-Pacific Partnership (TPP) for the pacific countries). Interesting innovations are present in a recent trade agreement signed between the European Union and Canada (CETA). The CETA commits the parties, with rather assertive language, to observe the fundamental principles and rules stated by the ILO conference of 1998, and also the right to strike (a rather unique case in trade agreements).

An innovative solution is provided concerning the procedures for the implementation of the social clause, which is usually the weakest part of trade agreements. The CETA establishes not only bilateral consultations among the parties aimed at resolving the disputes, like in most other agreements, but also a review panel of experts and civil society advisory groups entitled to submit opinions and recommendations. Moreover national labour inspectors are charged with controlling the implementation of the social clause. In case of non-acceptance of the judgment of the experts the claimant can suspend the obligations of the treaty of equivalent importance or ask for monetary compensation as indicated by the panel.

The CETA has set up a specialized tribunal composed of impartial members enabled to adjudicate the disputes with private investors arising under the treaty. This innovation is meant to correct the common procedures under the Investor-State Dispute Settlement (ISDS) clauses which have proved to be rather biased in favor of the investors.

Other Vehicles of Supranational Regulations: Codes of Conduct and Transnational Collective Agreements

Another set of supranational rules has been adopted by many multinational enterprises of European origin which have formalized codes of conduct referring to the fundamental rights and standards approved by the ILO. Similar codes are being adopted by multinationals of different nationalities. These codes have in common that they are legally non-binding, but they set guidelines to be observed by all the units of the company and of the enterprise group, including those operating in countries different from the home country. In some cases the respect of the guidelines is subject to external monitoring, but the independence of the monitoring is often uncertain. The effectiveness of the codes may depend on more than their legal force on the pressures of public opinion and of social organizations, which often denounce the violations of the codes and so put in danger the reputation of the company.[48]

Some European multinationals, influenced by the continental social model, have decided to consult the unions or to negotiate with them the content of the codes. In a few cases they have signed formal agreements with the European works councils which are the workers representative body present in many countries and promoted by a specific European directive (2009/38).[49]

The number of transnational agreements concluded with the works councils and with the unions has been growing.[50] These agreements have expanded their contents so as to improve the fundamental labour standards and to treat broad social and welfare issues.

The multiplication of these agreements has been favored by the trend to decentralize industrial relations to the company level, which is common to many countries, not only European countries. The accords concluded with the works councils may be more effective than the sectional agreements signed with the unions, because they can be implemented directly, also across borders, by the decision of the company which is party to the agreement. A limit of all these agreements is that they do not have a common legal status in the different European countries. Moreover, the employers' associations and the unions who sign the international agreements lack sufficient supranational powers to monitor and enforce them. This limit is common to the representative associations operating in most countries of the world.

The question of the legal enforcement of supranational agreements has received hardly any direct test, because the parties tend to solve the disputes arising under the agreement through their own channels (grievance procedures or the like). The national tribunals have been reluctant to decide labour cases arising in other countries, i.e. to admit an extraterritorial application of national labour laws.

A few pilot cases, mainly originated in the USA, are interesting as possible examples of a new courts attitude.[51] For example, a suit was brought by a Korean union against a firm for a dismissal decided in violation of a collective agreement and was taken to a court in New York where the mother company of the Korean firm was accused of interference with the local management. The court acknowledged the violation of the agreement, but did not sanction the mother company alleging a procedural exception. In spite of this unsatisfactory result the court decision many open the way to the possible enforcement of contractual obligations against multinational companies located in a country other than that where the violation occurred.

The enforcement may be easier when the supranational agreements are concluded by European multinationals operating in Europe. The courts of European states might be inclined to consider favorably cases concerning contracts or facts occurred in nearby countries, if somehow linked to events relevant to their territory, because they have been used to enforce regulations which derive from the authorities of the Union and which compose a supranational legal order. A recent example of the European supranational order comes from a directive, to be approved by the European Parliament, which is intended to fight social dumping among member states: a problem common to countries of other areas of the world.

The directive (96/71, to be revised) provides that the employees working in a place different from the home country of the employer are entitled to the same basic standards applied to the local employees (wages, social security, main working conditions).[52] The European interventions in favor of the member states is not limited to legal regulations such as the directives. Various forms of social policies, which are an expression of supranational solidarity are in place.

It is worth mentioning, in particular, that quite a few programs financed by European funds are aimed at responding to the most serious social problems present in Europe:[53] a program for supporting youth employment; many so-called "structural funds" aimed at promoting local development, particularly in the least developed areas; a special fund which can support financially and with personal assistance the employees who are "victims of globalization" (Reg. 1927/2006 instituting the FEG, 546/2009); the program "industry 4.0" which promotes private and public investments in technological innovation and in the necessary training of employees.[54]

These measures, which have been experimented in other regional areas, have proved useful in improving the relations among different nations, with concrete aids - financial and institutional. They have the advantage that can be implemented gradually and be adapted to the policy priorities of the interested communities.

A common limit of supranational rules depend on the fact that they are not sustained by the authority of state institutions and apparatus which have supported for centuries the binding effect of the law. The actors involved here are at least three: the international organizations, the national states, and the multinationals. The former institutions have no direct legislative powers and their enforcement mechanisms are largely dependent on national states and on social parties, which are reluctant to delegate to them more binding powers. The national states are still important actors, even though they are threatened by globalization. But so far they have not fully invested in supporting the implementation of supranational rules, particularly in employment and social matters. The multinational enterprises have acquired a major importance in international affairs and their influence is far greater than that exerted by the weak international projections of social parties, labour unions in particular. Moreover the regulation of social and employment relations is not the primary objective of these companies and is largely subtracted, independent from public influence.

Improving the quality and the effectiveness of transnational social regulations is not a merely technical task. It would require a change in the strategy of the various actors. The enterprises should accept more stringent social obligations than those resulting from the codes of practice. The states could require the enterprises to abide by the social standards included in the trade agreements and/or to give binding force to the principles of corporate social responsibility. But most important, they should give priority in their political agenda to supporting the influence of social rules in international relations.

Uncertain Prospects of Labour Regulations: The Role of the States and of the European Institutions

This brief overview of European experiences presents a very diversified scenario. Not only the specific measures, but the very approach to our discipline have profoundly changed in the last decade. In many cases the policy innovations have altered the fundamental traits of the established patterns of labour law and industrial relations. These changes contradict the widespread opinion that considers our discipline a sclerotic area of social sciences. The examples drawn from the various European countries confirm and indeed stress the diversity of the solutions adopted to meet the present challenges to the world of work. The diversity, even the polarization, between the various labour policies and regulations have significant influence on the national social and economic systems and may be considered as contributing to the varieties of capitalism. It is uncertain whether these innovations, even the most successful, will be sufficient to counteract the negative factors which have contributed to the decline of unions powers, of collective bargaining and to the weakening of labour rights. The evaluations by experts and politicians of the possible impact of these measures are divergent and not yet conclusive.

As I mentioned above they range from those which envisage a neoliberal convergence of most social and legal systems, which implies a reduced capacity to protect the rights of workers, to opinions which consider the present changes as a necessary adaptation of the traditional regulatory and welfare measures to new global and technological conditions. According to this latter opinion the legal and social innovations represent not a simple retrenchment, but a repositioning of our social and legal systems necessary to face the present challenges and to defend, if not all the acquired rights of the core workers, the essential standards of decent work for the persons who perform the various activities, often atypical, present in the mobile labour markets of today.

The implications of the measures implemented by the European states are also uncertain. Adopting different measures in the various countries, and even within the same country in the various economic sectors and areas, may be necessary to match the measures to the diversity of the factual conditions.[55] To some extent it may correspond to the increased complexity of our social and economic systems. But most critics emphasize the risk that this trend might lead to a stable dualism of legal and industrial relations regimes and contradict the mission of our discipline to promote social justice and progress for all workers and citizens. In any case, the examples presented here confirm the importance of the initiative of the national states and of the national social actors in determining the major trends of labour and industrial relations. Their strategies can make a difference, even in the present global scenario. Indeed some states are reasserting their authority in labour regulations and resisting the global pressures in response to the dangers of globalization.

The success of these initiatives will depend on the conditions of the various states, but also on their capacity to innovate the policy mix in the directions exemplified above: e.g. a more selective use of legislation concentrated on basic standard to be applied universally, a better balance between flexibility in the firms and security in the labour market, supported with active labour policies and income guarantees; increased investments in basic and digital education and in continuous training; promotion of worker participation in the enterprise and of union involvement in the administration of social security and placement services.

In Europe the institutions of the European Union have exerted significant influence also in the area of labour regulations and welfare, using many instruments, often indirect but more stringent than those available to other supranational and international institutions. The policies of the Union have been changing over the years. Recently, they have given priority to safeguarding financial stability with austerity measures even at the expense of policies necessary to support economic growth. The economic government of the European Union following this priority has influenced in various degrees the decisions of members states in economic and social matters. In the states most endangered by financial and economic crisis its decisions have severely limited the capacity to freely determine the most important public policies and have forced them to implement drastic forms of internal devaluation.

The reactions of the public opinion have provoked social and political repercussions in many countries (including the rise of anti-European movements). These reactions may have contributed to the recent proposals of the European Commission envisaging a reorientation of its priority toward growth-enhancing policies.[56] It remains to be seen if and to what extent this new approach will materialize and will produce significant changes in labour policies and regulations. Even experts not prejudiced against the Union are skeptical, and forecast that further inertia of the European institutions may contribute to the revival of nationalism in labour regulations.

I am convinced that labour regulations are an important element of the social order. If framed well they can positively contribute to economic competitiveness and to sustainable development. But as already mentioned good regulations and social policies are only one contributing factor to this end. The whole range of public policies must be finalized to the objective of creating a more inclusive and sustainable growth. The economic and financial strategies adopted by the states and by the European Union will have a decisive influence also on our field.

Notes

1 Baccaro, L. and Howell, C. (2011) "A Common Neoliberal

Trajectory. The Transformation of Industrial Relations in Advanced Capitalism," *Politics and Society*, 3, pp. 521-563, and lately Baccaro, L. and Howell, C. (2018) *The Trajectories of Neoliberal Transformation*, Cambridge University Press.

2 See the preoccupied remarks by Clarke, L., Donnelly, E., Hyman, R., Kelly, J., McKay, S. and Moore, S. (2008) *What's the Point of Industrial Relations?*, paper presented to the British Universities Industrial Relations Association Conference (BUIRA) at the University of the West of England, June 26-28, 2008; the authors believe in the fundamental role of our discipline as a critical social science, for the improvement of the employment conditions and the promotion of social progress.

3 The ISLSSL has launched seven comparative research groups at the World Congress of the Cape Town of September 2015.

4 See similar remarks in Gumbrell-McCormick, R. and Hyman, R. (2016) *Trade Unions in Western Europe: Hard Times, Hard Choices*, Oxford University Press, p. 6; Lehndorff, S., Dribbush, H. and Schulten, T. (eds.), (2017), *Rough Waters European Trade Unions in a Time of Crisis*, ETUI, p. 14ff.

5 The term "model" is commonly used, but must be taken in a rather loose and non-normative sense, since it does not exclude variations in the legal regulations and in the social policies adopted by the various countries.

6 The constitutional recognition of these rights has contributed to diffuse their application in the member states: see Barnard, C. (2013) *The Charter, the Court and the Crisis*, Legal Studies Research Papers series, 48, University of Cambridge; Giubboni, S. (2005) *Social Rights under the European Constitution: Comparing Ideal-typical Models of European Constitutionalism*, WP M. D'Antona, INT. 29/2005, ID, (2011) "Social Europe after the

Labour Treaty, Some Skeptical Remarks," *European Journal of Social Law*, p. 246ff.

7 A multi-level perspective is necessary to grasp the complex reality of labour and of employment relations. The regulations themselves have become multi-level. See Lansbury, R. *The International Labour and Employment Relations Association (ILERA) at Fifty: The Journey so Far and the Way Ahead*, paper for this Congress and Chapter 7 in this volume.

8 Similar conclusions in Pedersini, R. (2014) "European Industrial Relations between Old and New Trends," in *Stato Mercato*, p. 345ff. The reflection paper on the *Social dimension of Europe*, of the European Commission COM (2013) 206-207, admits that "divergences" persist.

9 The role of the state in Industrial Relations is the theme of research group n. 7 of the ISLSSL.

10 This point is stressed by Weiss, M. *Challenges for Labour Law and Industrial Relations*, Chapter 6 in this book.

11 Verma, A. *The Challenge of Labour Regulation in the Era of Globalization*. Paper presented in this Congress.

12 See my remarks in *Labour Law and Social Policies: An Agenda for Transnational Research*, presented at the 21st World Congress of ISLSSL, Cape Town (2015), WP, M. D'Antona, INT 128/2016. Atypical types of work are spreading in different forms both in advanced and emerging countries; often their informality escape the traditional controls of the law and borders on illegality. These issues are analyzed in research group n. 1 of the ISLSSL.

13 Industrial Relations in Europe, 2014-2015, according to the data of the average rate of unionization has decreased from 27% of 2000 to 23.4% of 2008.

14 Pedersini, R. "European Industrial Relations between Old and New Trends," p. 345ff. Visser, J. (2015) *Database 5.0*, Amsterdam Institute for advanced labour studies, AIAS.

15 See for data and comments Pedersini, R. "European Industrial Relations between Old and New Trends," p. 344ff.

16 See e.g. Auer, P. and Cares, S. (eds.), (2003) "Introduction," in *Employment Stability in the Age of Flexibility*, ILO; see also *Reconciling Labour Flexibility with Social Cohesion*, Council of Europe Publishing, Strasbourg, 2006.

17 See the first proposals by Wilthagen, T. (2004) "Flexicurity: A New Approach to Regulating Employment and Labour Markets," in *Transfer*, 10(2), pp. 166-186; Muffels, R. and Whiltagen, T. (2013) "Flexicurity: A New Paradigm for the Analysis of Labour Markets and Policies Challenging the Trade-off between Flexibility and Security," in *Sociology Compass*, 7(2), pp. 111-122; Communication from the Commission to the European Parliament, the Council, the European Economic and Social Committee and the Committee of the Regions, June 27, 2007, COM (2007) 359 final.

18 See the critical analysis of Muffels, R., Crouch, C. and Whiltagen, T. (2014) "Flexibility and Security: National Social Models in Transnational Labour Markets," in *Transfer*, 20(1), 102ff.

19 See Mandl, I. and Celikel-Esser, F. (2012) *The Second Phase of Flexicurity, An Analysis of Practices and Policies in the Member States*, Eurofound, 18ff and 73.

20 The various practices are presented in the Eurofound analysis, *The Second Phase of Flexicurity*.

21 See the Italian ACT 81/2015 (art. 3).

22 See the research group n. 6 of the ISLSSL.

23 Hemerjick, A. (2013) *Changing Welfare State*, Oxford University Press, p. 133ff.; Ferrera, M. (2005) T*he Boundaries of Welfare: European Integration and the Spatial Policies of Social Protection*, Oxford University Press; Cantillon, E.B. (2011) "The Paradox of Social Investment: Growth, Employment and Poverty in the Lisbon Era," *Journal of European Social Policy (JESP)*, p. 432ff.

24 European Economic and Social Committee 2017, I*mpact of Digitalization and on Demand Economy on Labour Market and the Consequences for Employment and Industrial Relations* (www.eesc.Europa.eu).

25 OECD, The future of work, Policy Forum, January 2016; S. Scarpetta, *The Future of Work*, Conference INAPP, ANPAL, CNEL, November 9, 2017 (www.CNEL.it).

26 See the document of the European trade Unions Institute, *The Why and How of Working Time Reduction*, ETUI, 2017.

27 OECD, Skills for a digital work 2016, Policy brief on the *Future of Work*.

28 See the remarks by Weiss, M. "Challenges for Labour Law and Industrial Relations," Chapter 6 in this book.

29 The Italian Act 15/2015 revising art. 4 of Act 300/1970, and the Code on data protection (Act 196/2003).

30 See a recent discussion of the various forms of workers participation in Perulli, A. (2017) "Introduction" to Perulli, A. and Treu, T. *Enterprise and Social Rights*, Wolters Kluwer, p. 1ff.; and the chapters in this volume by Weiss, M. "Workers Participation in the Enterprise, in Germany," p. 293ff.; Treu, T. "Workers Participation in the Firm, Trends and Insights," p. 271ff.

31 In Italy Act 208/2015 and similar subsequent provisions.

32 See Hepple, B. and Veneziani, B. (2009) *The Transformation of*

Labour Law in Europe, a Comparative Analysis. Hart Publishing; Ales, E., Deiuert, O. and Kenner, J. (eds.), (2017) *Core and Contingent Work in the European Union, a Comparative Analysis, Hart Publishing; New Forms of Employment,* Eurofound 2015, Luxembourg.

33 ILO, Recommendation 2015 (n. 204), Transition from the informal to the formal company.

34 This type of work has attracted a great number of legal analysis: see e.g. Cherry, M.A. (2011) "A Taxonomy of Virtual Works," in *Georgia Law Review,* 45, p. 951; Degryse, C. (2016) *Digitalization of the Economy and Its Impact on Labour Markets,* working papers, 2; De Stefano, V. (2014) *The Rise of the Just in Time Workforce: On Demand Work. Crowdwork and Labour Protection in the Gig Economy,* in ILO. Working Papers, Conditions of working series, n. 71; Prassl, J. and Risak, M. (2016) "Uber, TaskRabbit and Co.: Platforms as Employers? Rethinking the Legal Analysis of Crowdwork," in *Comparative Labour Law and Policy Journal,* 37, p. 619; Davidov, G. (2017) "The Status of Uber Drivers: A Purposive Approach," in *Spanish Labour Law and Employment Relations Journal,* 6(1-2); Eurofound (2017) *Working Anytime, Anywhere. The Effects on the World of Work*(www.eurofound.Europa.eu/publications/report/2017/working- anytime-anywhere-the-effects-on-the-world-of-work).

35 See, e.g. Rogers, B. (2016) "Employment Rights in the Platform Economy: Getting Back to Basic," in *Harvard Law and Policy Review,* 10, p. 479; Cherry, A.M. (2016) "Beyond Misclassification: The Digital Transformation of Work," in *Comparative Labour Law and Policy Journal,* 37, p. 577.

36 Escande-Varniol, M.C. (2017) *What Protection for Workers Acting via Digital Platform in a Market Economy?,* paper draft,

Toronto Seminar; Jeammaud, A. (2017) "Uber, deliveroo: requalification des contracts ou dénonciation d'une fraude à la loi," Semaine Sociale Lamy, 1780, September 4, p. 4ff.

37 Case C. 434/15, Associacion professional Elite Taxi v. Uber system Spain, December 20, 2017.

38 See Industrial Relations in Europe, 2014-2015, Schulten, B. (2016) *The Meaning of Extension for the Stability of Collective Bargaining in Europe*, ETUI, Policy Paper 4; Visser, J. (2016) "What Happened to Collective Bargaining During the Great Recession," IZA, *Journal of Labour Policy*, 5(9); Bordogna, L. and Pedersini, R. (2015) "What Kind of Europeanization? How EMU is Changing Industrial Relations in Europe?," DLRI, p. 183ff.

39 In general Schulten, J. and Muller, I. (2014) *Back on the Agenda: An European Minimum Wage Standard*, ETUI, Policy Brief, n. 8.

40 In general industrial relations in Europe, 2014-2015, and in Japan: Araki, T. (2017) "Japan's Decentralized Industrial Relations, Internal Flexicurity and Challenges Japan Faces," in A. Perulli-T. Treu, *Enterprise and Social Rights*, p. 173ff.

41 See the Combrexelle Report, *La negociacion collective, le travail et l'emploi*, France Strategie, 9 sett. 2015; Ray, E. (2015) *Droit du travail, droit vivant*, Wolters Kluwer, p. 688.

42 Magnani, M. *The Role of Collective Bargaining in Italian Labour Law*, paper presented to the World Congress of comparative law to be held, July 2018, at Fukuoka, Japan.

43 The importance of "organizing" the process of decentralization is recognized by many industrial relations scholars: see Crouch, L. and Traxler, F. (eds.), (1995) *Organized Industrial Relations in Europe: What Future?*.

44 Visser, J. (2004) *Recent Trends and Persistent Variations in Europe's Industrial Relations*, Dutch Social and Economic Council, EIRO, www.ser.nl; Hyman, R. (2010) *Social Dialogue and Industrial Relations During the Economic Crisis Innovative Practice or Business as Usual*, ILO, Geneva, work paper; Hassel, A. (2010) "Twenty Years after German Unification," in *German Politics and Society*, 7; Glassner, V. and Keune, M. (2010) *Negotiating Crisis? Collective Bargaining in Europe during the Economic Downturn*, WP, 11, ILO, Geneva. Critical remarks in Bisbinck, R. and Dribbugh, H. (2011) *Collective Bargaining and Crisis Management in the German Metalworking Industry Since 1990*, WSK Discussion Paper, Dusseldorf, p. 177.

45 The importance of innovative managerial practices capable of promoting so-called high-road strategies is stressed by Kochan, T. "Challenges and Opportunities Facing ILERA and our Field," Chapter 3 in this book.

46 See, in general, Bellace, J.R. (2014) "Human Rights at Work: The Need for Definitional Coherence in the Global Governance System," in *International Journal of Comparative Labour Law and Industrial Relations*, 30(2), pp. 175-198; Compa, L. (1998) "The Multilateral Agreements on Investment (MAI) and International Labour Standards: A Failed Connection," in *Cornell International Law Journal*, 31, pp. 683-712; Compa, L. and Vogt, J. (2003) "Labour Rights in the Generalized System of Preferences: A 20 Year Review," in *Comparative Labour Law and Policy Journal*, 22, pp. 199-238; Ebert, F. and Posthuma, A. (2011) "Labour Provisions in Trade Arrangements Current Trends and Perspectives," *International Institute for Labour Studies*, discussion paper series; Perulli, A. and Treu, T. *Enterprise and Social Rights*.

47 Faioli, M. (2015) "The Quest for a New Generation of Labour Chapter in the TTIP," in *Economia & Lavoro*, 49, pp. 103-120; European Parliament, *TTIP and Jobs*, Directorate general for international policies, Policy Department, 2016.

48 Blanpain, R. (1979). *The OECD Guidelines Per Multinational Enterprises and Labour Relations*, Kluwer, and reviews 1983 and 1985; Tergeist, P. (2014) "Multinational Enterprises and Codes of Conduct: The OECD Guidelines for MNEs in Perspective," in Blanpain, R. *Comparative Labour Law and Industrial Relations in Industrialized Market Economies*, Kluwer, p. 213ff.

49 Waddington, J., Putignano, V. and Turk, J. (2016) *Managers Business Europe and the Development of European Works Council*, ETUI, working paper.

50 Ales, E. et al. (2006), *Transnational Collective Bargaining. Past, Present and Future*, final report, European Commission; Casale, G. (2017) "Collective Bargaining at Transnational Level," in Perulli, A. and Treu, T. (2017) *Enterprise and Social Rights*, Wolters Kluwer, p. 161ff. See the analyses of research group n. 5 of the ISLSSL.

51 See Compa, L. (2002) "Pursing International Labour Rights in US Courts, New Uses for Old Tools," in *Industrial Relations*, 57(1), p. 48ff.

52 Davies, P. (1997) "Posted Workers: Single Market or Protection of National Labour Law System?," *Common Market Law Review*, p. 571ff.

53 In the use European Funds in general, *The Social Investment Package*, Communication of the EU Commission, (COM 2013) 83 final. Particularly important for our field is the European Social Fund now regulated by reg. 1303 and 1304/2013.

54 In the use European Funds in general, *The Social Investment*

Package, Communication of the EU Commission, (COM 2013) 83 final. Particularly important for our field is the European Social Fund now regulated by reg. 1303 and 1304/2013.

55 Verma, A. *The Challenge of Labour Regulation in the Era of Globalization.*

56 *The European Pillar of Social Rights*, November 2017, COM (2017) 250 final, COM (2017) 251 final; see also ILO, *Building a Social Pillar for European Convergence*, July 2016.

References

Ales, E., Jaspers, A.Ph.C.M., Engblom, Samuel, Laulom, Silvana, Sobczak, André, Valdés Dal Ré. (2006) *Transnational Collective Bargaining. Past, Present and Future*, final report, European Commission.

Ales, E., Deiuert, O. and Kenner, J. (eds.), (2017) *Core and Contingent Work in the European Union, a Comparative Analysis*, Hart Publishing.

Araki, T. (2017) "Japan's Decentralized Industrial Relations, Internal Flexicurity and Challenges Japan Faces," in Perulli, A. and Treu, T. *Enterprise and Social Rights*, Wolters Kluwer.

Auer, P. and Cares, S. (eds.), (2003) "Introduction," *Employment Stability in the Age of Flexibility*, ILO.

Baccaro, L. and Howell, C. (2011) "A Common Neoliberal Trajectory. The Transformation of Industrial Relations in Advanced Capitalism," *Politics and Society*, 3, pp. 521-563.

Baccaro, L. and Howell, C. (2018) *The Trajectories of Neoliberal Transformation*, Cambridge University Press.

Barnard, C. (2013) *The Charter, the Court and the Crisis*, Legal Studies Research Papers series, 48, University of Cambridge.

Bellace, J.R. (2014) "Human Rights at Work: The Need for Definitional Coherence in the Global Governance System," *International Journal of Comparative Labour Law and Industrial Relations*, 30(2), pp. 175-198.

Bisbinck, R. and Dribbugh, H. (2011) *Collective Bargaining and Crisis Management in the German Metalworking Industry Since 1990*, WSK Discussion Paper, Dusseldorf.

Blanpain, R. (1979) *The OECD Guidelines Per Multinational Enterprises and Labour Relations*, Wolters Kluwer.

Bordogna, L. and Pedersini, R. (2015) "What Kind of Europeanization? How EMU is Changing Industrial Relations in Europe?," DLRI.

Cantillon, E.B. (2011) "The Paradox of Social Investment: Growth, Employment and Poverty in the Lisbon Era," *Journal of European Social Policy (JESP)*.

Cherry, M.A. (2011) "A Taxonomy of Virtual Works," *Georgia Law Review*, 45.

Cherry, A.M. (2016) "Beyond Misclassification: The Digital Transformation of Work," *Comparative Labour Law and Policy Journal*, 2016, 37.

Clarke, L., Donnelly, E., Hyman, R., Kelly, J., McKay, S. and Moore, S. (2008) *What's the Point of Industrial Relations?*, paper presented to the British Universities Industrial Relations Association Conference (BUIRA) at the University of the West of England, June 26-28.

Communication from the Commission to the European Parliament, the Council, the European Economic and Social Committee and the Committee of the Regions, June 27, 2007, COM (2007) 359 final.

Compa, L. (1998) "The Multilateral Agreements on Investment (MAI) and International Labour Standards: A Failed Connection,"

Cornell International Law Journal, 31, pp. 683-712.

Compa, L. (2002) "Pursing International Labour Rights in US Courts, New Uses for Old Tools," *Industrial Relations*, 57(1).

Compa, L. and Vogt, J. (2003) "Labour Rights in the Generalized System of Preferences: A 20 Year Review," *Comparative Labour Law and Policy Journal*, 22, pp. 199-238.

Council of Europe, (2006) *Reconciling Labour Flexibility with Social Cohesion*, Council of Europe Publishing, Strasbourg.

Crouch, L. and Traxler, F. (eds.), (1995) *Organized Industrial Relations in Europe: What Future?*, Avebury.

Davies, P. (1997) "Posted Workers: Single Market or Protection of National Labour Law System?," *Common Market Law Review.*

Davidov, G. (2017) "The Status of Uber Drivers: A Purposive Approach," *Spanish Labour Law and Employment Relations Journal*, 6(1-2).

Degryse, C. (2016) *Digitalization of the Economy and Its Impact on Labour Markets*, working papers.

De Stefano, V. (2014) *The Rise of the Just in Time Workforce: On Demand Work. Crowdwork and Labour Protection in the Gig Economy*, ILO.

Ebert, F. and Posthuma, A. (2011) "Labour Provisions in Trade Arrangements Current Trends and Perspectives," *International Institute for Labour Studies*, discussion paper series.

Escande-Varniol, M.C. (2017) *What Protection for Workers Acting via Digital Platform in a Market Economy?*, paper draft, Toronto Seminar.

Eurofound, (2017) *Working Anytime, Anywhere. The Effects on the World of Work* (www.eurofound.Europa.eu/publications/report/2017/working-anytime-anywhere-the-effects-on-the-world-of-work).

European Economic and Social Committee (2017) *Impact of*

Digitalization and on Demand Economy on Labour Market and the Consequences for Employment and Industrial Relations (www. eesc. Europa. eu).

European Parliament (2016) *TTIP and Jobs*, Directorate general for international policies, Policy Department.

European Trade Unions Institute (2017) *The Why and How of Working Time Reduction*, ETUI.

Faioli, M. (2015) "The Quest for a New Generation of Labour Chapter in the TTIP," *Economia & Lavoro*, 49, pp. 103-120.

Ferrera, M. (2005) *The Boundaries of Welfare: European Integration and the Spatial Policies of Social Protection*, Oxford University Press.

Giubboni, S. (2005) *Social Rights under the European Constitution: Comparing Ideal-typical Models of European Constitutionalism*, WP M. D'Antona.

Giubboni, S. (2011) "Social Europe after the Labour Treaty, Some Skeptical Remarks," *European Journal of Social Law.*

Glassner, V. and Keune, M. (2010) *Negotiating Crisis? Collective Bargaining in Europe during the Economic Downturn*, WP, 11, ILO.

Gumbrell-McCormick, R. and Hyman, R. (2016) *Trade Unions in Western Europe: Hard Times, Hard Choices*, Oxford University Press.

Hassel, A. (2010) "Twenty Years after German Unification," *German Politics and Society*, n. 7.

Hemerjick, A. (2013) *Changing Welfare State*, Oxford University Press.

Hepple, B. and Veneziani, B. (2009) *The Transformation of Labour Law in Europe, a Comparative Analysis*, Hart Publishing.

Hyman, R. (2010) *Social Dialogue and Industrial Relations During the Economic Crisis Innovative Practice or Business as Usual*, ILO, Geneva, work paper.

ILO (2016) *Building a Social Pillar for European Convergence*, July.

Jeammaud, A. (2017) "Uber, Deliveroo: Requalification des contracts ou dénonciation d'une fraude à la loi," *Semaine Sociale Lamy*, 1780, September 4.

Labour Law and Social Policies: An Agenda for Transnational Research (2015) presented at the 21st World Congress of ISLSSL, Cape Town.

Lehndorff, S., Dribbush, H. and Schulten, T. (eds.), (2017) *Rough Waters European Trade Unions in a Time of Crisis*, ETUI.

Mandl, I. and Celikel-Esser, F. (2012) *The Second Phase of Flexicurity, An Analysis of Practices and Policies in the Member States*, Eurofound.

Mandl, I., Curtarelli, M., Riso, S., Vargas Llave, O. and Elias, G. (2015) *New Forms of Employment*, Eurofound, Luxembourg.

Muffels, R., Crouch, C. and Whiltagen, T. (2014) "Flexibility and Security: National Social Models in Transnational Labour Markets," *Transfer*, 2014, 20(1), 102ff.

Pedersini, R. (2014) "European Industrial Relations between Old and New Trends," *Stato Mercato.*

Perulli, A., (2017) "Introduction," in Perulli, A. and Treu, T. *Enterprise and Social Rights*, Wolters Kluwer.

Perulli, A. and Treu, T. (2017) *Enterprise and Social Rights*, Wolters Kluwer.

Prassl, J. and Risak, M. (2016) "Uber, TaskRabbit and Co.: Platforms as Employers? Rethinking the Legal Analysis of Crowdwork," *Comparative Labour Law and Policy Journal*, 37.

Ray, E. (2015) *Droit du travail, droit vivant*, Wolters Kluwer.

Rogers, B. (2016) "Employment Rights in the Platform Economy: Getting Back to Basic," *Harvard Law and Policy Review*, 10.

Scarpetta, S. (2017) *The Future of Work*, Conference INAPP, ANPAL, CNEL, November 9 (www.CNEL.it).

Schulten, B. (2016) *The Meaning of Extension for the Stability of Collective Bargaining in Europe*, ETUI, Policy Paper 4/2016.

Schulten, J. and Muller, I. (2014) *Back on the Agenda: An European Minimum Wage Standard*, ETUI, Policy Brief, n. 8/2014.

The European Pillar of Social Rights, November 2017, COM (2017) 250 final, COM (2017) 251 final.

The Social Investment Package, Communication of the EU Commission, (COM 2013) 83 final.

Tergeist, P. (2014) "Multinational Enterprises and Codes of Conduct: The OECD Guidelines for MNEs in Perspective," in Blanpain, R. *Comparative Labour Law and Industrial Relations in Industrialized Market Economies*, Wolters Kluwer.

Treu, T. (2017) "Workers Participation in the Firm, Trends and Insights," Perulli, A. and Treu, T. *Enterprise and Social Rights*, Wolters Kluwer.

Visser, J. (2004) *Recent Trends and Persistent Variations in Europe's Industrial Relations*, Dutch Social and Economic Council.

Visser, J. (2015) *Database 5.0*, Amsterdam Institute for advanced labour studies, AIAS.

Visser, J. (2016) "What Happened to Collective Bargaining During the Great Recession," IZA, *Journal of Labour Policy*, vol. 5, n. 9.

Waddington, J., Putignano, V. and Turk, J. (2016) *Managers Business Europe and the Development of European Works Council*, ETUI, working paper.

Weiss, M. (2017) "Workers Participation in the Enterprise, in Germany," Perulli, A. and Treu, T. *Enterprise and Social Rights*, Wolters Kluwer.

Wilthagen, T. (2004) "Flexicurity: A New Approach to Regulating Employment and Labour Markets," *Transfer*, 10(2), pp. 166-186.

The West and the East in Industrial Relations and Labour Law

Tadashi Hanami[1]

06

Universal Wisdom Through Globalization

The title of my Presidential Address for the 12th World Congress of the IIRA in Tokyo was "Universal Wisdom through Globalization." In that address I touched upon the question of whether industrial relations in the world are "convergence or divergence" based on the papers submitted to this Congress.[2] It has been quite obvious that the industrial relations and labour laws in non-Western countries were formulated based on the Western model simply because these countries were latecomers in terms of modern economies. A few years before the 2000 Tokyo Congress, three "officers" of the IIRA (M. Weiss, A. Valdez and myself) took the initiative of publishing a 50-year history of the IIRA. As a result of this idea, a book titled *The Global Evolution of Industrial Relations - Events, Ideas and the IIRA* was written by Bruce E. Kaufman and published by ILO in 2004. However, it was interesting to find that almost all of the pages in this 722-page publication were exclusively dedicated to descriptions of Western industrial relations. More than 400 pages from Chapter 2 to Chapter 9 were spent on describing industrial relations and labour in North America, Australia, the UK and other European countries. In Chapter 10, only about 50 pages were dedicated to discussing industrial relations in Africa, Asia and Latin America.

As far as the description of individual countries in this book are concerned, 15 pages are dedicated to each Germany and Japan, 6 pages for France and India, a mere 4 pages for Israel and a little more than 2 pages for Korea, Nigeria and South Africa.

Western Domination in the Industrial Relations and Labour Law Field of Study

This unbalanced distribution precisely reflects the interests of world scholars in the field of labour in spite of a strong emphasis on globalizing trends in general. Today after nearly two decades since the publication of this rather comprehensive academic work, it is very significant that another World Congress is going to be hosted in Asia for the first time since the Tokyo Congress in 2000. I very much wish and expect that a good part of the discussions will be dedicated to the study of development in the Eastern hemisphere during each session of this Congress.

Recent Changes Taking Place in the Western Hemisphere

However, in terms of globalization, from a broader perspective, it is interesting to find that a lot of remarkable new phenomena have emerged in the Western world within the past 18 years since the time of the Tokyo Congress; not only in terms of politics and economics, but also with regard to culture and society in general.

For instance, it is interesting to find that The New York Times (International ed.) of April 5, 2018, published only a few days prior to this writing, published two lengthy articles titled "How democracy became the enemy" by Roger Cohen and "Can we stop fascism, or is it too late?" by Madeleine Albright which covered almost two full pages of the internationally prestigious newspaper. Again, about a week later, the same newspaper (April 14-15) published another interesting article entitled "In Germany, a resurgence of the right" by Anna Sauerbrey and "A renaissance on the right" by David Brooks. Especially, David Brooks (2018) pointed out that "Suddenly fundamental issues, like the values of the liberal democratic order itself, are up for debate. Some conservatives are laying down comprehensive critiques of the way our society is organized." Such journalistic trends in the Western world are a rather a significant phenomenon in the sense that they illustrate the concept of a "paradise lost" in the West. Meanwhile, in this context, it is also interesting to observe that "populism" in the field of politics and "neo-orientalism" in terms of idea and thought are also emerging in the Western hemisphere.

Populism in the West

The concept of "populism" in recent political theory is defined as a "political movement" based on an opposition between the "elite" and the "common people." Emerging populism in this sense is regarded as "political movement from below against the elite and the establishment."[3] In the recent few years we have seen such a confrontation between the "common people" and the establishment. This kind of confrontation has been emerging in the activities of populist parties in many European countries in connection with growing questions about the function of EU mechanisms as they relate to processes such as Brexit. The opposition of the "lower class" against the "establishment/elites" was also observed in the election of US President Trump in 2016.

Most populist parties have self-appointed their political orientation as the "harbingers" of "genuine democracy" representing the "underdog common people" against the "established elite class." Populism in this sense often furthers the narrative that the established elites have been promoting globalization, European integration and policies of tolerance for immigration and, as a result, neglecting the interests of the "under" class of ordinary people. Populism claims to directly represent the "people" against the establishment.

Margaret Canovan distinguished between two patterns of "democracy," (1) "pragmatic democracy" and (2) "redemptive democracy." In "pragmatic democracy," conflict resolution takes place by introducing rules and systems, emphasizing daily routine administrative processes while in redemptive democracy the direct participation of the "people" is more emphasized. It is very interesting, particularly from the viewpoint of a specialist in the field of industrial relations and labour, to observe the recent trend, at least in the European context, where the power of trade unions and farmers' organizations have been constantly and drastically declining. Organization rates of trade unions in Western countries has been constantly declining in recent decades from around 30 to 10% with the exception of a few Scandinavian countries.

It is quite natural that major established political parties such as the social-democrats or the Christian democrats are closely connected with working-class organizations (such as trade unions and farmers' associations) and are regarded as representative of "their" established interests while populists tend to be perceived as representing "our" interests. Thus, the disconnection and severance of establishments and privileged elites has provided an effective background for criticism by populists in major European countries such as France, Austria and Belgium. These three countries share a number of common features such as (1) active exploitation of mass media, (2) direct democracy, (3) "Welfare chauvinism," (4) origin of "extreme rights" (5) anti-immigration and anti-Islam sentiment.

The election of Donald Trump as US president is also regarded as an emergence of a sort of populism on the other side of the Atlantic Ocean. It is pointed out that there exists a common factor between the "abandoned" people of the Rust Belt in the United States and the neglected poor in Great Britain who supported Brexit.

Post-orientalism in the West

In connection with the above-mentioned emergence of populism in Western countries in the recent decades, the birth of "post-orientalism" is another significant phenomenon. Of course "post-orientalism" is a newly emerged thought and idea introduced by Hamid Dabashi as a reconsideration and forward step to "orientalism" which itself was first created by Edward Said (an American thinker of Palestinian origin).[4] Dabashi pointed out that Western journalism tends to continue to associate Arabs with terrorism, especially after 9/11. According to him, the imbalance between the West and non-West has been expanding more and more with the development of global capitalism. The non-West continued to resist this disregard and neglect by the West and has so resisted by exchanging information and stories in their own voice with each other. Nevertheless, those who listen to these stories (or not) have always been in the West. In this controlling structure the West has always been the subject/center and the non-West object/outsider.

This strategy proposed by Dabashi is unique in the sense that those controlled by the West exchange their local stories and wisdom with each other and get together in a global context. In this context it is important to mention the significant decline in the role of established international organizations such as the UN, UNESCO, ILO etc. which were established and controlled by the Western establishment. It is about time that all ruled and oppressed non-westerners exchange their local stories, information and wisdom with each other on a global scale.

In connection with the above-described newly emerging global trends, we can expect a great deal of meaningful discussions to take place based on the good number of papers and presentations which will be submitted to this World Congress taking place in Asia for the first time in 19 years since the 2000 Congress in Tokyo.

Notes

1 This chapter was submitted to ILERA World Congress, 2018.

2 Universal Wisdom Through Globalization, Selected Papers from 12th IIRA World Congress. Tokyo, the Japan Institute of Labour, 2002.

3 Canovan, Margaret (1999) "Trust the People! Populism and the Tow Faces of Democracy," *Political Studies*, 47(1), pp. 2-16.

4 Dabashi, Hamid (2009) *Post-Orientalism Knowledge and Power in Time of Terror*, Transaction Publishers.

References

Albright, Madeleine (2018) "Can We Stop Fascism, Or Is It Too Late?," *The New York Times*, April 7/8.

Brookes, David (2018) "A Renaissance on the Right," *The New York Times*, April 12 (https://www.nytimes.com/2018/04/12/opinion/renaissance-right-gop.html).

Canovan, Margaret (1999) "Trust the People! Populism and the Tow Faces of Democracy," *Political Studies*, 47(1), pp. 2-16.

Cohen, Roger (2018) "How Democracy Became the Enemy," *The New York Times* (https://www.nytimes.com/2018/04/06/opinion/Sunday/orban-hungary-kaczynski-poland.html).

Dabashi, Hamid (2009) *Post-Orientalism Knowledge and Power in Time of Terror*, Transaction Publishers.

Sauerbrey, Anna (2018) "In Germany, a Resurgence of the Right," *The New York Times* (https://www.nytimes.com/2018/04/13/opinion/german-conservatism-comeback.html?searchResultPosition=1).

Challenges for Labour Law and Industrial Relations

Manfred Weiss

07

Introduction

"Beyond Traditional Employment. Industrial Relations in the Network Economy" was the general topic of the 13th World Congress of ILERA (then still IIRA), organized in Berlin 2003 in the period of my presidency. The issues discussed there are as important today as they were then. This applies to the track "Enterprise Reorganisation: Negotiated, Consultative or Unilateral" as well as to the track "Changing Contours of the Employment Relationship and the New Models of Labour Regulation," "Industrial Relations and Global Labour Standards," "Collective Actors in Industrial Relations: What Future?"

The problems implied by the fragmentation and segmentation of the workforce were discussed as well as the ongoing erosion of the traditional enterprise by outsourcing, networking and similar strategies in the context of a globalized economy. The decline of standard employment in favor of new forms of work was analyzed as well as the increasing difficulty of identifying the employer in scattered enterprise structures. The limits and weaknesses of international labour regimes were subject to debate as well as the increasing difficulties for trade unions to organize collective power, particularly in the international arena.[1]

The topics to be discussed and the problems to be resolved have remained the same up to now. But they have become more complex and more dramatic today than at the turn of the century. The promotion and enforcement of global labour standards has remained an unresolved problem which particularly becomes evident in view of the increasing phenomenon of global supply chains. And the technological development has changed the world of work in a way that urgently new answers on how to cope with this challenge are to be found.

It, of course, will not be possible in this contribution to present a comprehensive overview on all the challenges labour law and industrial relations are facing in this globalized economy, and in view of the latest technological developments. Therefore, I will limit myself to indicate just some unresolved problems in reference to international labour standards (in the next section) and in reference to digitalization of work (in the section titled: "Impact of Digitalization on Labour Law and Industrial Relations"). My intention is not to present possible solutions, but rather to identify the challenges, the obstacles for solutions and the uncertainties on how to cope with these challenges. Or to put it differently: I would like to sketch some problems for future activities of ILERA.

The Deficiencies of International Regulation

The Enforcement Problem

In a globalized economy it is possible for the transnationally operating companies to shift production and services to countries with lowest labour standards and, thereby, lowest labour costs. This leads to social dumping between countries. In order to turn around this run to the bottom it is necessary to establish a worldwide minimum floor of protection. This task evidently cannot be achieved by national law. It needs international norm setting. The International Labour Organization (ILO) and to a certain extent also the United Nations (UN) have been involved in developing international labour standards in order to achieve this ambitious goal.

Above all the UN and the ILO have developed social human rights which are supposed to be the point of reference for labour law, worldwide. They are embedded in the UN Universal Declaration on Human Rights of 1948 (Art. 23 and 24), in the UN International Covenant on Economic, Social and Cultural Rights of 1966 (Art. 6-8) and in the ILO Declaration of 1998 on Core Labour Rights. In addition the ILO has passed almost 200 Conventions on all aspects of Labour Law and Social Security. In short, there is already an impressive set of universal minimum labour standards.

The problem is less the production of norms[2] than the lack of implementation in practice and in particular the lack of enforcement mechanisms. This applies to all the UN instruments. The ILO conventions suffer not only from an often low level of ratification[3] but, in particular, from a rather toothless monitoring system. Even if the influence of the case law of the different monitoring bodies of the ILO on the judicial debates in member countries cannot be denied, this is by far not enough. The ILO standard setting machinery needs significant strengthening. As far as monitoring and sanctioning are concerned, the system of the European Convention on Human Rights where conflicts are adjudicated by the powerful European Court of Human Rights might serve as a model for more efficient enforcement of conventions. However, a consensus for such a structure on a global scale is not easily achieved. Many obstacles would have to be surmounted. Attempts to establish the Tribunal which is envisaged in Art. 37 par. 2 of the ILO constitution failed. The majority of the

Member States are unwilling to increase the ILO's power to enforce their norms.

For a long time it was taken for granted that it is up to the supervising committees of the ILO, the Committee of Experts as well as the Committee on Freedom of Association, to interpret the vague notions of the conventions and, thereby, to specify the scope and the content of the conventions. This traditional view has now been contested. At first glance the controversy is only on the right to strike. However, the right to strike was only the occasion, whereas the impact of the controversy goes far beyond it.

The situation is becoming even worse. It started with a conflict on the right to strike. The right to strike is not mentioned in ILO Convention 87. But the committees of the ILO supervisory system from the very beginning and for decades took the position that the right to strike is implied by Art. 3 of Convention 87 and they specified it in their case law. This was accepted by the employers' representatives in the ILO, in particular for the fact that in the communist Member States strike was forbidden. Thereby, the legitimacy of communism could be attacked. When the Berlin Wall and the Iron Curtain fell, this attitude of the employers' camp started to change. The controversy escalated when in 2012 the employers refused to sign the list of Member States violating the right to strike. The employers' group not only insisted on the wording of Convention 87 but declared that the respective committees had no mandate to decide anything, that their work only would be for internal purposes of the ILO and would have no external effect whatsoever. This conflict is not settled yet.[4] In a tripartite conference in 2015 a sort of cease fire was reached by a joint declaration of the representatives of the trade unions and employers' associations. For a preliminary period the employers' side agreed to cooperate as before. But this is neither a final agreement on the right to strike nor on the mandate of the committees. Theoretically and according to the constitution of the ILO there would be a possibility to bring the conflict before the International Court in The Hague. This, however, is very unlikely. Each side is afraid of a definitive judgment. Where the conflict finally will end up is an open question.

Can Private Actors Compensate the Enforcement Deficiency?

In view of the indicated enforcement problem the question arises whether the assistance of private actors might fill the gap between the international labour standards as law in the books and real efficient factual implementation. Already, many decades ago the ILO and the Organization for Economic Cooperation and Development (OECD) tried to take use of the fact that the Multinational Enterprises (MNE) might be able to define the context in which they are active. The OECD guidelines for MNE as well as the Tripartite Declaration of Principles on Multinational Enterprises and Social Policy, both of the mid-seventies of last century and until today often revised and amended, were passed to initiate such a supplementary task for the MNE. And in the turn of the century they were complemented by the UN's "Global Compact" which serves the same goal. These "external" guidelines were mainly meant to enrich the fantasy of management in the MNE in elaborating so-called private codes of conduct. Such codes have become numerous and are mainly a product of the last decades.

Even if these codes are by no means homogeneous,[5] they all refer to the core fundamental rights as contained in the ILO Declaration of 1998. For the rest there are big differences between them. Even more significant are the differences between different branches of activity. Some codes simply refer to the whole set of ILO standards. The codes not only are very different in reference to their content but also in their genesis. Most of the codes are unilaterally established by the companies. However, to an increasing extent there is a new generation of codes called "multi-stakeholder" initiatives. Human rights groups, community and development organizations participate in formulating such codes of conduct.[6] These "multi-stakeholder codes" contain also provisions on monitoring, verification, certification of supplier factories, enforcement mechanisms and transparency. In the meantime the certification industry has grown enormously.

All these codes are legally non-binding. They are "light touch" regulations or "soft law." There is only a moral obligation by the MNE to respect them. In case of unilaterally developed codes the companies are very much interested in internal conflict resolution. Therefore, in these cases the outside observers do not learn anything about possible violations. However, there are MNE who want to make perfectly clear that they are not interested in hiding violations. They have decided to be exposed in regular intervals to so-called "external monitoring." This of course applies - as already mentioned - to all "multi-stakeholder codes" of the new generation.

However, this certification business should not be overestimated, in particular since the certifying agencies are paid by the MNE. The main purpose of such certificates in the meantime has become widely used as a marketing strategy. "Social labeling" plays an ever bigger role.

One of the weaknesses of the codes of conduct is the exclusion of the trade unions as an actor. Or to put it differently: codes of conduct to a great extent are to be understood as a strategy to escape the trade unions. Exactly this deficiency is supposed to be overcome by a new strategy: the International Framework Agreements (IFA).

IFA are the result of direct negotiations between the headquarters of the MNE and Global Union Federations (GUF).[7] The negotiations take a rather long time, in general between one and three years. The IFA are a phenomenon which really started only in the first decade of the twenty-first century. Mainly two developments within the international trade union camp made this new strategy possible: the transformation of the former International Trade Secretariats (ITS) into GUF and the merger of the two largest international confederations, the International Confederation of Trade Unions (ICFTU) and the World Confederation of Labour (WCL) into the single International Trade Union Confederation (ITUC) in 2006. However, compared to codes of conduct the number of IFA is still relatively small.

Even if the IFA comes closest to a traditional understanding of industrial relations, they should not be confused with traditional collective agreements concluded by the two sides of industry in a domestic context. They do not specify in detail terms and conditions of employment, but rather set a framework for the relationship between the MNE and the trade unions, the workers, again quite often throughout the whole supply chain. The GUF and the MNE function in this context not so much as classical bargaining parties but rather as civil society actors shaping and channeling "culture" as a catalyst both for change in mentalities and subsequently for the formulation of relevant public policies and laws.[8]

IFAs are a new quality compared to codes of conduct with which they should not be confused. Whereas codes of conduct to a great extent were intended to escape any engagement with trade unions, the GUF and their affiliates in the different countries are now recognized as partners with whom arrangements are to be made.

It is of utmost importance that IFAs contain a machinery of joint monitoring which generally introduce joint monitoring committees that consist of management and worker representatives and that are intended to meet regularly in order to assess progress or deal with conflicts. The GUF cooperates closely with national trade unions in implementing IFAs. The more this interaction works, the better the effects. Monitoring by trade unions is a new quality compared to the monitoring systems in the context of codes of conduct. The employee delegation in these joint monitoring bodies usually comprises company-level representatives and a representative from the GUF and from the union of the company's home country.

The question, how efficient these mechanisms are in actual practice, has become a most interesting topic of empirical studies. Presently quite a few research projects are focusing on the factual implementation of IFAs. Therefore factors that support the intended effects as well as factors that prevent such a development can be identified.

The spill-over effects of IFAs should not be underestimated. IFAs have led already to the establishment of a significant number of company-based bodies of interest representation as well as to the promotion of social dialogue and cooperation which support the development of mutual trust. And there is no doubt that the efforts to negotiate an IFA and to implement them have a significant impact on the structure of the GUF, on their interaction with national trade unions and on the transnational perspective of the trade union movement as a whole.[9]

Nevertheless, even behind this promising strategy remains a big question mark, in particular since after a promising start, unfortunately, stagnation will be observed. It seems that the enthusiasm for IFAs already has more or less come to an end. Therefore, private activities in the context of the MNE only to a very limited extent can be considered as compensation for the diagnosed enforcement deficiency of international labour standards.

Fear of Binding Rules: the Example of Global Supply Chains (GSC)

One of the most burning problems is the lack of decent labour standards in GSC[10] and in particular the lack of liability of the headquarters of MNE in cases where in the worldwide supply or value chain, employees suffer damages because international labour standards are violated, as had happened in the well-known Rana Plaza case in Bangladesh where in April 2013 more than 1,000 workers were killed and many more injured.

This tragic event served as a wake-up call, at least for better protection of health and safety. The main result was the conclusion of the Accord on Fire and Building Safety in Bangladesh less than one month after the event on May 15, 2013. It is a legally binding agreement between, at present, more than 200 MNE and trade unions and is designed to build a safe and healthy Bangladeshi Ready Made Garment (RMG) Industry. It contains a comprehensive and efficient program for prevention of accidents, for sanctions in cases of violations and for remedies for those who suffer damages. It expired in May 2018. Only after lengthy controversial debates - the Rana Plaza shock is no longer present - an extension for three more years has been reached.

The Accord could serve as a model for the regulation of GSC. However, it only refers to health and safety and covers only one industry in one country. This evidently is, by far, not enough. A much more comprehensive regulation covering all countries and all branches where GSC are active and covering other important topics (wage, working time etc.) is needed.

At least as health and safety is concerned an attempt of extension to other branches and countries has been made. In October 2015 the G7 States introduced the Vision Zero Fund (VZF). It strives to realize the goal of zero-work-related fatalities and severe injuries and diseases by improving occupational health and safety practices and conditions in all sectors linked to GSC and beyond Bangladesh all over the world. The fund also seeks to strengthen institutional frameworks such as labour inspectorates and employment injury insurance schemes in countries linked to GSC.

An interesting attempt to strive for comprehensive regulation for GSC took place in the UN Human Rights Council (HRC), established in 2006 and made up of 47 Member States. In 2014 the HRC passed a resolution for elaborating a binding instrument. This resolution was initiated by Ecuador and South Africa. It was backed by a big majority of mainly developing countries, whereas the industrialized countries, among them Germany, France, UK, Italy, Japan, South Korea and USA, voted against. The advantages of such an instrument compared to the guiding principles would be mainly three: (a) it would be an international solution with universal obligations for the Member States and indirectly for the companies; (b) it would be a uniform solution in reference to companies' responsibilities, sanctions, access to remedies, enforcement etc. and (c) it would be legally binding. A working group has been established. It meets in regular sessions, but the chances for a satisfying result tend toward zero.

At least the HRC's initiative has led to the fact that "Decent Work in GSC" became a topic on the agenda of the ILO's International Labour Conference (ILC) of 2016, based on a report of the International Labour Office.[11] The trade union delegates were pleading for a convention on this subject which, however, was strongly rejected by the employers' camp. The result of this debate are joint conclusions on the lowest common denominator. The ILO was asked to develop a legally non-binding action plan on how to promote decent work in supply chains and companies are encouraged to conduct "Human Rights Due Diligence." This soft law approach has been confirmed in the ILC session 2017.

Evaluation

There is a significant amount of international regulation, social human rights and rules for all kinds of labour law aspects. However, there is a lack of implementation. It still is mainly law on the books and not law in actual practice, at least not to a sufficient extent. Voluntary codes of conduct do not lead to a significant change. IFA concluded between the headquarters of MNE and GUF might be a step forward, but their increase is more than uncertain.

There is consensus that GSC are problematic and improvement of working conditions is indispensable. In the area of health and safety some progress has been made. All attempts to elaborate legally binding international instruments have failed so far. Everything remains on the level of soft law, low pressure and voluntary activity. There is not much hope that this will change in the near future. The ILERA might act as a pressure group in this context to promote ideas on how to overcome the indicated deficiencies.

Impact of Digitalization on Labour Law and Industrial Relations

The Different Types of Digital Work

Digitalization of working patterns has many faces, it is not to be conceived as a uniform or homogeneous phenomenon. Many details are still rather unclear. But undoubtedly it means, as well as globalization, a dramatic transformation of the world of work. Each of the different working patterns leads to different implications for labour law and industrial relations. Three types are most relevant in this context.

Already for several decades communication technologies made it possible for work not to have to be performed in the premises of the employer but can be executed anywhere. The labels used for this type of work are "telework" or "mobile work."[12]

Another trend of this digital evolution is labeled "industry 4.0" which stands for the Fourth Industrial Revolution.[13] The label is somehow misleading because this type of work not only refers to manufacturing, but also in the same way to services. Collaborative robots become intelligent, which means they are able to adapt, communicate and interact. Smart robots communicate with each other and with humans on interlinking tasks. These cyber-physical systems are quickly widening, including various functions in production, logistics or office management.

The third important trend is the increasing platform economy[14] where a crowd-sourcer launches a call or competition on an online platform, gathers proposals from the crowd and evaluates the proposals to select the proposal deemed most suitable for the intended purpose. Here basically two types are to be distinguished: "internal platforms" to which only the workforce of a specific company has access and "external platforms" with open access for anybody meeting specific criteria. Among the "external platforms" again two types are to be distinguished: "work on demand via app" where the work is performed in a traditional way (transport, cleaning etc.) and "online crowd-work" where work is performed by a crowd-worker online. Again platforms must be distinguished between platforms where relatively simple tasks are performed by unskilled or low-skilled persons and complex platforms where highly skilled persons are confronted with complex tasks.

There is no doubt that at least to a certain extent human beings will be substituted by robots, thereby losing their jobs. The challenge will be to keep the number of these people as small as possible and to re-skill those who are substituted in order to re-integrate them into the labour market. The even bigger challenge, however, will be whether and how the work in view of digitalization can be regulated in a way which will guarantee that the traditional goals of labour law to protect the worker, to respect his or her dignity, in particular to guarantee his or her privacy as well as his or her physical, mental and psychological health.

The problem to be sketched in this contribution is the impact these developments have on traditional labour law and industrial relations. How these challenges can be met, is still rather uncertain. The purpose of this contribution is to briefly indicate the direction in which regulatory strategies might be developed.[15]

Growing Importance of Training

As indicated, a main effect of digitalization will be that the content of work will be very different compared to today and that other skills will be needed. Therefore, one implication of the new scenario is certain: lifelong learning will play a much bigger role than ever. Vocational training will have to be directed much less to specific skills and functions, but to the ability on how to learn and how to adapt to new circumstances. It will be necessary to be much more focused on training than ever before. Work has to be accompanied by ongoing training of the workforce. Labour law has to provide the framework for such skilling opportunities. Workers must get the time and the resources to engage in continuous learning processes. Not only governments, but also the actors in collective bargaining as well as the actors in workers' participation schemes are confronted with this task. Joint efforts of all these actors are needed. In Germany the metal workers trade union at least in one branch have already succeeded in concluding a collective agreement providing space and financial resources for such educational efforts. This is only a small beginning, but it shows the direction which will have to be followed.

Reconsideration of the Scope of Labour Law Protection

Already for quite a long time it has become evident that the demarcation line between employment and self-employment is very difficult to draw.[16] To an increasing extent there are persons labeled as being self-employed, but in reality they are actually employees. They of course are to be included into the scope of application of labour law, even if it might be difficult to exactly identify their status. Problematic are those who undoubtedly are self-employed, but economically in a similar position as employees. Therefore, in many countries a specific category has been invented for the economically dependent self-employed. In Germany they are called "employee like persons." However, only some rules of labour law are applied on them. The reason is very simple: if they are only economically but not personally dependent, their situation remains distinguishable from employees in a strict sense.[17]

This well-known problem will further increase in the era of digitalization. The degree of autonomy in performing work makes it more and more difficult to categorize the persons involved in such work. Many of those who participate in crowdsourcing certainly are not employees but rather self-employed. So far, neither minimum wage rules nor health and safety standards apply to them. Or let's take the well-known system established by Uber to illustrate the problem. Customers use an app on their smartphones to request rides from a specific location. This information is instantly broadcasted to the drivers in the area. The driver who accepts the request is directed to the passenger and onwards to the required destination through the Uber app. Payment is taken automatically from the customer by the platform and after the deduction of a commission passed on to the driver. The drivers are rated afterwards by the customers.[18] It has become extremely controversial whether these drivers are employees, thereby covered by labour law, or whether they are self-employed. Answering this question is very difficult. Courts all over the world have been busy deciding this question. Quite a few lawsuits are still pending in many countries.

The problem to be resolved goes far beyond the outcomes of these lawsuits. There is growing consensus that the traditional demarcation line between employment and self-employment no longer makes sense. It does not fit into the reality of digital work. But the direction of the reform is still very controversial. One possibility might be a re-conceptualization of the notion of employee, thereby widening the scope of labour law protection. Another possibility might be the introduction of an intermediary category between employment and self-employment as it is already the case in quite a few countries. A more radical possibility would be the inclusion of self-employed up to a certain wage level into the protective roof of labour law. Finally, it might be considered to develop special regulations for work in the context of platforms or at least for crowd-workers.[19]

Each of these possible solutions has to cope with severe difficulties and uncertainties. In each case demarcation lines have to be drawn to fit an ever-changing reality: a giant task. And it is more than doubtful whether it makes sense to extend the whole protective scheme of labour law (and also social security law) to groups who so far fall under the category of self-employed. But then the question arises: what kind of protection (and to what extent) is needed for which categories? This question is closely linked to the problem whether protective standards taking account of the specific situation of workers in platform contexts might be the same as for other economically dependent self-employed or whether they have to be different. And would special rules have to be continuously adapted in view of exponential technological development? There are many unresolved questions; no satisfying answers are in sight.

The platform economy is not only an attack on the concept of employee but also on the concept of employer. To again take the example of Uber it might be helpful to have a look into the terms and conditions where the customers are informed that they "acknowledge that Uber does not provide transportation or logistics services or function as a transportation carrier," but merely as an agent between driver and customer. It might be doubtful whether and in how far such structures fit into the traditional concept of employer. Therefore, a big debate on re-conceptualization of this notion has started, trying to develop a functional concept of employer, fitting better into the reality of platform economy and making it more difficult for a platform to escape their duties.[20]

Reconsideration of Working Time

As indicated above digitalization will focus more on goals to be achieved in a certain time frame. Presence at the workplace will be less important. How and when within the given time frame the work is to be performed is more or less left to the discretion of the worker. This "autonomy" leads to the question whether traditional working-time regulations still are appropriate to cope with this situation. Working-time regulation so far has focused mainly on daily and weekly maximum working time, on breaks and rest periods between the days and providing holidays and vacations. Step-by-step flexibility has been built in. Daily and weekly maximum working time could be exceeded to a certain extent if compensated by reduction of working time within a certain period. However, in spite of the flexibility element, working-time regulation still remains rather rigid.

In the digital world there is the danger that working time never ends. Workers may be assumed to remain online and to answer e-mails and phone calls also after normal working time as well as on holidays and on vacations. And even if the workers are not asked by the employer to do so, they might do it voluntarily. This has far-reaching implications on health and safety of the workers as well as on their private life. Relaxation and rest, as it is supposed by traditional working-time regulation, is no longer possible under these conditions. Self-exploitation is an ever increasing danger. The eight-hour day, the big achievement of the labour movement in the early twentieth century is in danger of being abolished.

The question is whether regulations are possible at all. The blocking of access to crowd-platforms for specific hours might not be very helpful, because the crowd-workers might still continue working on their projects and put the results later on the platform. In Germany some companies have concluded with the works councils agreements according to which the servers are disconnected after a certain time of the day and during the weekend and employees are not to be called. During vacations the account for the respective worker is to be blocked. Therefore, the employee enjoys the right to non-availability. This shows a way of working in the right direction. It, however, only can be a first step. Not all employees are happy with such a regulation, some are afraid of the increased workload they are confronted with after the periods of disconnection.

Things are even more complicated when workers are involved in production or service processes with workers in other time zones. Then such disconnection might be counter-productive. In short and to make the point: the traditional working-time regulation is no longer feasible but an appropriate alternative is not yet in sight.

Growing Importance of Data Protection

As indicated the possibility of collecting and evaluating data by digital tools will increase dramatically. This means that the worker privacy will be more endangered than ever. It cannot be left to the discretion of the employer regarding what data are collected, stored and connected with other available data.

However, not only the workers' privacy is at stake. It also has to be made sure that business secrets are not endangered. This is further complicated by the fact that more and more often workers are supposed to use their own devices for professional purposes (smartphones, tablets etc.). As a consequence, not only are business secrets and client confidentiality endangered, quite a few problems arise in the relationship between employers and workers. Can the employer dispose of the worker's private property? Can the employer prohibit the worker's devices from also being used by other people or that cloud services are used? And what about monitoring if business data and private data both are on such devices? Can the worker be obliged to report to the employer if his or her smartphone is lost or stolen? All these questions indicate that the policy of "bring your own device (BYOD)" leads to a whole set of further unresolved problems.

Reconsideration of Health and Safety

Digitalization will make it necessary to totally rethink the concept of health and safety. The traditional focus on physical dangers has to be radically changed towards psycho-social problems.

It is already common knowledge that the danger of psycho-social disorders has significantly increased in the information society. This will further increase if, to a greater extent, work is characterized by technology-driven forms of work. De-localization, the decreasing relevance of traditional working-time patterns, the focus on work results to be produced in a certain period and no longer on presence at the workplace as well as the loss of clear-cut hierarchies promotes worker autonomy which is considered to promote creativity and innovation. In reality this new autonomy is very ambiguous, it implies the danger of self-exploitation. This implies a need for new patterns of stress prevention and new strategies on how to cope with the consequences of stress. How this can be regulated, is an open question and a big challenge for all the actors of industrial relations.

New Concept of Work-Life Balance

So far, labour law has tried to develop patterns which make it possible to find a better balance between work and private life, family obligations etc. Part-time work, parental leave or leave for care of sick or elderly family members are well-known examples of such a policy. However, these strategies all were developed under the assumption that work and private life are two different entities. This distinction, more and more, may fall apart due to digitalization of work. De-localized work and work without clear time limits is increasingly intruding into private life, thereby eliminating to a greater extent the demarcation line between the two spheres of human life. This not only will have a significant impact for family life, but for society as a whole. It, again, is an open question whether, in how far and by what kind of regulation the private part of life can be rescued.

Growing Difficulties of Collective Representation

The traditional Fordist model was characterized by a relatively homogeneous workforce in a hierarchically structured factory or office. As already indicated above, this model became ineffective with the segmentation and fragmentation of the workforce, which are divided in core groups and non-standard groups with significantly diverse interests. This trend is dramatically increased by the digitalization of work. The example of the platform workers shows that there is no longer a connection between the acting individuals;

they do not know each other and work in splendid isolation.

Technological innovation cycles by digitalization of work are becoming faster and faster. The legislator will not be able to keep up with the changes and adapt the rules to the respective needs. The legislator only can provide a relatively flexible framework. Solutions balancing the needs of the platforms and the workers are to be developed on a decentralized level, be it in the area of training, of working time, of health and safety or of data protection. These solutions cannot be left unilaterally to the employer but must be developed in cooperation with representative bodies of the workforce. In other words, the working conditions are to be shaped and monitored together with the employees' representatives, be it by way of information and consultation or even by co-determination. "Co-operative turn" has become the catchword for this approach.

The difficulties for worker participation, of course, have not only grown due to digitalization. Outsourcing and networking strategies have made it more and more difficult to identify the employer. However, these difficulties, as indicated above, have significantly grown in the platform economy.

The basic requirement for worker participation, be it via institutionalized schemes or be it by collective bargaining, is the possibility to develop collective structures among digital workers, in particular in the context of platforms. Whether this goal can be achieved or whether it remains to be an illusion in the digital economy is still an open question. But, there is no doubt that the answer to it will decide the future development and the sustainability of digital work.

The first step to be taken in this direction is to overcome worker unanimity and isolation.[21] A group of trade unions from different countries have already started to devote themselves to this task. To just give an example: representatives from trade unions in Austria, Denmark, Germany and the United States of America as well as from the Service Employees International Union met in Frankfurt, Germany in April 2016 together with an international group of industrial relations experts to discuss possible strategies. This resulted in a joint declaration on platform-based work.[22] Therein they explained "the possibilities for a 'co-operative turn' in labour-management relations in the 'platform economy', in which workers, clients, platform operators, investors, policy makers, and worker organizations work together to improve outcomes for all stakeholders." And they identified platform providers as "appropriate negotiating partners for platform-based workers seeking to improve their conditions of work," even if in some cases "clients may also be appropriate negotiating partners." In particular they insisted that "all workers on the platform regardless of whether they are employees or independent contractors" are to be included in "a platform's policies and information flows." And as far as the "co-operative turn" is concerned the declaration reads as follows:

> The 'traditional' conflictual processes of labour-management relations have secured crucial rights for workers over the years and will continue to be important. But insofar as platform operators understand that their long-term well-being, and that of society at large is bound up with the ability of workers - regardless of their status - to secure good work, future labour-management interactions may be organized around interests deeply shared by all parties. This possibility offers the hope of great gains for all parties.

This optimistic view was not only accompanied by a list of topics to be regulated (wages, social protection etc.) but in particular by a request for two strategies which might serve as a first step on the way to a "co-operative turn": establishment of transparency and a mechanism for dispute resolution.

It is stated in detail that to a great extent the whole operation of platforms remains in the dark. This refers to processes for assigning tasks, the preconditions for account closure or computing worker reputation and other qualifications, to just mention some examples. Complaints refer to the fact that often the use of platforms is obscured by posting tasks under wrong names. The declaration resumes that "in short, the knowledge base required to make sound policy is missing." Therefore, transparency is understood to be the indispensable precondition to develop a strategy for the collective voice of platform workers.

As far as dispute resolution is concerned, the declaration proposes "that platform operators work - with workers, clients, researchers, worker organizations, and other actors as appropriate - to develop transparent, accountable methods for resolving disputes between clients and workers, and, as needed, between workers." In this context it may be of interest that in November 2017 the German Metalworkers' Union "IG Metall" together with the German Crowd-sourcing Association and eight important crowd-working-platforms established an Ombudsman's Office,[23] composed of an equal number of platform representatives on the one side and representatives of "IG Metall" and crowd-workers on the other side, chaired by a judge of the Frankfurt labour court. It is supposed to mediate conflicts between crowd-workers, platforms and clients and to monitor compliance with a code of conduct on which the participating platforms, in 2015, agreed as a form of voluntary self-regulation. The code was amended in 2017.[24]

This code of conduct contains 10 principles to be respected by the platforms offering only: lawful tasks, information of the crowd-workers on the legal framework for their work, fair wages, user-friendly and motivating working conditions, respectful behavior between platforms, clients and crowd-workers, freedom of crowd-workers to accept or refuse offers without fear of negative consequences, constructive feedback and open communication, transparent procedure of acceptance of work results by the platform and finally protection of personal data and privacy. All these details are further described and explained in order to make them workable tools.

At the same time IG Metall has established a platform where crowd-workers can communicate with each other and where the trade union can communicate with them. The idea is to, thereby, overcome the anonymity and isolation in order to create a collective consciousness as a basis for collective organization and collective action. To further promote this goal IG Metall also conducts workshops with crowd-workers and platform representatives at regular intervals.

Whether such initiatives will be successful in building up a collective structure remains to be seen. They are nothing but first steps. But at least it shows that trade unions are taking efforts to promote such a development. Of course, such efforts cannot remain limited to national contexts since crowd-workers of platforms may come from several countries. However, the already mentioned fact that trade unions in these efforts cooperate transnationally is a promising sign.

Whether the big majority of crowd-workers may be able to develop collective power is to be doubted. The big majority are low-skilled workers performing simple tasks. They easily can be substituted, which evidently has a negative impact on their bargaining power. Therefore, not too much should be expected. This, however, might be very different where complex tasks by highly skilled workers are performed. It might be quite difficult to substitute them, which definitely increases their bargaining power. The problem might be whether solidarity between them can be established since within the platforms, most of the time, they are competitors. In short, and to make a point, there are promising steps to overcome the isolation of crowd-workers. Only the future will tell where they end up. Again, it is a challenge for ILERA to contribute to this development and, thereby, to make sure that crowd-workers have a chance to work under decent working conditions.

Conclusion

These sketchy remarks may leave us very frustrated given lots of challenges and no feasible solutions up to now. As far as globalization is concerned, social human rights and international labour standards have to be strengthened. In particular, the enforcement machinery has to be improved. And, as the example of GSC demonstrates, the willingness of those countries who profit from unequal labour conditions to support decent regulation has to be promoted. The question in reference to digitalization will be - to put it in a somehow pathetic formula - whether labour law, the legislator and the collective actors will succeed to make sure that human beings will not be the slaves of this new technological phenomenon. It is the task of labour law and industrial relations scholars as well as of practitioners in the field to make sure that the latter alternative will become reality. Digitalization contains many risks, but it also is a chance to improve working and living conditions to the benefit of workers. It is not an apocalyptic evil but something which needs to be shaped. And definitely it can be shaped if all actors involved are committed to do it. The ILERA is the ideal forum to cope with all these challenges. If the topic of last year's World Congress in Seoul asked what is to be done for employment for a sustainable society, these challenges might provide some food for thought.

Notes

1 For these debates see Rymkewitch, O. (2004) 13th World Congress of the International Industrial Relations Association (IIRA), in *The International Journal of Comparative Labour Law and Industrial Relations (IJCLLIR)*, pp. 305-310.

2 For a comprehensive overview on the ILO's standard setting activities see Rubin, N. (ed.), (2005) *Code of International Law*, 2 volumes, Cambridge.

3 See Hepple, B. (2005) *Labour Law and Global Trade*, Hart Publishing, p. 35.

4 For this conflict see Hofmann, C. (2014) *(The Right to) Strike and the ILO - Is the System for Monitoring Labour and Social Standards in Trouble?*, Friedrich Ebert Foundation.

5 For an illustration of the big variety of codes see Scherrer, C. and Greven, T. (2001) *Global Rules for Trade: Codes of Conduct, Social Labeling Workers' Rights Clauses*, Muenster; Webb, K. (ed.), (2003) *Voluntary Codes, Private Governance, the Public Interest and Innovation*, Carleton Research Unit for Innovation, Science and Environment, Carleton University.

6 For details of this development see Compa, L. (2008) Corporate Social Responsibility and Workers' Rights, *Comparative Labour Law and Policy Journal*, pp. 1-10 (pp. 5-10).

7 For an interesting account of this development see Drouin, R.C. (2010) "Promoting Fundamental Labour Rights through International Framework Agreements: Practical Outcomes and Present Challenges," *Comparative Labour Law and Policy Journal*, pp. 591-636.

8 For the practical implications see Schoemann, I. (2011) "The Impact of Transnational Company Agreements on Social Dialogue

and Industrial Relations," in Papadakis, K. (ed.), *Shaping Global Industrial Relations. The Impact of International Framework Agreements*, Geneva, pp. 21-37.

9 See Papadakis, K., Casale, G. and Tsotroudi, K. (2008) "International Framework Agreements as Elements in a Cross-border Industrial Relations Framework," in Papadakis, K. (ed.), *Cross-Border Social Dialogue and Agreements: An Emerging Global Industrial Relations Framework?*, Geneva, pp. 67-88.

10 For an assessment of the problems see Lee, J. (2016) *Global Supply Chain Dynamics and Labour Governance: Implications for Social Upgrading*, ILO Research Paper No. 134, Geneva.

11 www.ilo.org/ilc/ILCSessions/105/reports/reports-to-the-conference/WCMS_468097/lang--en/index.htm

12 For the problems arising in the context of telework see the contributions in Blanpain, R. (ed.), (2007) "European Framework Agreements and Telework - Law and Practice, A European and Comparative Study," *Bulletin of Comparative Labour Relations*, 62; Mella Méndez, L. (ed.), (2015) *Trabajo a Distancia Y Teletrabajo*, Cazur Menor.

13 Almada-Lobo, F. (2016) "The Industry 4.0 Revolution and the Future of Manufacturing Execution Systems (MES)," *Journal of Innovation Management*, 16-21.

14 For the different types of work in the platform economy see De Stefano, V. (2016) "Introduction: Crowdsourcing, the Gig-Economy and the Law," *Comparative Labour Law add Policy Journal*, pp. 461-470.

15 For a good overview on this debate see Liebman, W. (2017) *The Gig Economy, Crowdwork and New Forms of Work*, Soziales Recht, pp. 221-238.

16 See for a comprehensive discussion of this problem Davidov, G.

and Langille, B. (eds.), (2006) *Boundaries and Frontiers of Labour Law*, Hart Publishing; for an interesting proposal on how to overcome it Freedland, M. and Kountouris, N. (2011) *The Legal Construction of Personal Work Relations*, Oxford University Press.

17 See Waas, B. (2017) "Crowdwork in Germany," in B. Waas et al., *Crowdwork - A Comparative Law Perspective*, Bund-Verlag GmbH, pp. 142-186 (pp. 160-162).

18 For a very good illustration for such rating systems see Silberman, M. and Irani, L. (2016) Operating an Employer Reputation System: Lessons from Turkopticon 2008 - 2015, *Comparative Labour Law and Policy Journal*, pp. 505-541.

19 For the difficulty of categorization see Aloisi, A. (2016) "Commoditized Workers: Case Study Research on Labour Law Issues Arising from a Set of 'On Demand/Gig Economy' Platforms," *Comparative Labour Law and Policy Journal*, pp. 653-690.

20 Prassl, J. and Risak, M. (2016) "Uber, Taskrabbit, and Co.: "Platforms as Employers? Rethinking the Legal Analysis of Crowdwork," *Comparative Labour and Policy Journal*, pp. 619-651; Prassl, J. and Risak, M. (2017) "Working in the Gig Economy - Flexibility Without Security?," in Singer, R. and Bazzani, T. (eds.), (2017) *European Employment Policies: Current Challenges*, Berliner Wissenschafts-Verlag, pp. 67-95.

21 See the report on developments in the USA by Liebmann, W. "Crowdworkers, the Law and the Future of Work: The U.S.," in B. Waas et al., op.cit., pp. 24-141 (pp. 115-127).

22 www.igmetall.de/docs_20161214_Frankfurt_Paper_on_Platform_Based_Work_EN_

23 www.igmetall.de/docs_2017_11_8_Presseinformation_ Ombudsstelle Crowdworking_ef5ebcd3b52f834a38b64ec80377aee518d11009.pdf

24 www.igmetall.de/begruessenswerte-entwicklung-im-crowdsourcing-24652.htm

References

Almada-Lobo, F. (2016) "The Industry 4.0 Revolution and the Future of Manufacturing Execution Systems (MES)," *Journal of Innovation Management*, pp. 16-21.

Aloisi, A. (2016) "Commoditized Workers: Case Study Research on Labour Law Issues Arising from a Set of 'On Demand/Gig Economy' Platforms," *Comparative Labour Law and Policy Journal*, pp. 653-690.

Blanpain, R. (ed.), (2007) "European Framework Agreements and Telework - Law and Practice, A European and Comparative Study," *Bulletin of Comparative Labour Relations* 62.

Compa, L. (2008) "Corporate Social Responsibility and Workers' Rights," *Comparative Labour Law and Policy Journal*, pp. 1-10.

Davidov, G. and Langille, B. (eds.), (2006) *Boundaries and Frontiers of Labour Law*, Hart Publishing.

De Stefano, V. (2016) "Introduction: Crowdsourcing, the Gig-Economy and the Law," *Comparative Labour Law add Policy Journal*, pp. 461-470.

Drouin, R.C. (2010) "Promoting Fundamental Labour Rights through International Framework Agreements: Practical Outcomes and Present Challenges," *Comparative Labour Law and Policy Journal*, pp. 591-636.

Freedland, M. and Kountouris, N. (2011) *The Legal Construction of Personal Work Relations*, Oxford University Press.

Hepple, B. (2005) *Labour Law and Global Trade*, Hart Publishing.

Hofmann, C. (2014) *(The Right to) Strike and the ILO - Is the System for Monitoring Labour and Social Standards in Trouble?*, Friedrich Ebert Foundation.

Lee, J. (2016) *Global Supply Chain Dynamics and Labour Governance: Implications for Social Upgrading*, ILO Research Paper No. 134, Geneva.

Liebman, W. (2017) *The Gig Economy, Crowdwork and New Forms of*

Work, Soziales Recht, pp. 221-238.

Liebmann, W. (2017) "Crowdworkers, the Law and the Future of Work: The U.S.," in Waas, B, Liebman, Wilma B., Lyubarsky, Andrew and Kezuka, Katsutoshi (eds.), Crowdwork - *A Comparative Law Perspective*, Bund-Verlag GmbH.

Mella Méndez, L. (ed.), (2015) *Trabajo a Distancia Y Teletrabajo*, Cazur Menor.

Papadakis, K., Casale, G. and Tsotroudi, K. (2008) "International Framework Agreements as Elements in a Cross-border Industrial Relations Framework," in Papadakis, K. (ed.), *Cross-Border Social Dialogue and Agreements: An Emerging Global Industrial Relations Framework?*, Geneva, pp. 67-88.

Prassl, J. and Risak, M. (2016) Uber, Taskrabbit, and Co.: "Platforms as Employers? Rethinking the Legal Analysis of Crowdwork," *Comparative Labour and Policy Journal*, pp. 619-651.

Prassl, J. and Risak, M. (2017) "Working in the Gig Economy - Flexibility Without Security?," in Singer, R. and Bazzani, T. (eds.), *European Employment Policies: Current Challenges*, Berliner Wissenschafts-Verlag, pp. 67-95.

Rubin, N. (ed.), (2005) Code of International Law, 2 volumes, Cambridge.

Rymkewitch, O. (2004) 13th World Congress of the International Industrial Relations Association (IIRA), *The International Journal of Comparative Labour Law and Industrial Relations (IJCLLIR)*, pp. 305-310.

Schoemann, I. (2011) "The Impact of Transnational Company Agreements on Social Dialogue and Industrial Relations," in Papadakis, K (ed.), *Shaping Global Industrial Relations. The Impact of International Framework Agreements*, Geneva, pp. 21-37.

Scherrer, C. and Greven, T. (2001) *Global Rules for Trade: Codes of Conduct, Social Labeling Workers' Rights Clauses*, Muenster.

Silberman, M. and Irani, L. (2016) "Operating an Employer Reputation

System: Lessons from Turkopticon 2008 - 2015," *Comparative Labour Law and Policy Journal*, pp. 505-541.

Waas, B. (2017) "Crowdwork in Germany," in Waas B., Liebman, Wilma B., Lyubarsky, Andrew and Kezuka, Katsutoshi (eds.), *Crowdwork - A Comparative Law Perspective*, Frankfurt, pp. 142-186.

Webb, K. (ed.), (2003) *Voluntary Codes, Private Governance, the Public Interest and Innovation*, Carleton Research Unit for Innovation, Science and Environment, Carleton University.

The International Labour and Employment Relations Association (ILERA) at 50: The Journey So Far and the Way Ahead

Russell D. Lansbury

08

In this chapter, I will reflect on the history of ILERA and its possible future by drawing on my personal involvement in ILERA and its predecessor (IIRA) since attending the second World Congress in 1970. I will divide the development of ILERA during the past 50 years into three phases in order to chart the changes which have occurred since its foundation to the present time. I will then discuss the changing nature of labour and employment relations (ER), particularly with the impact of globalization. I will argue for a multi-institutional perspective which emphasizes the importance of interaction between different spheres of work and ER. Finally, I will offer some suggestions about the role that ILERA might play in encouraging and facilitating the development of ER as an area of study and its application now and into the future.

The Formative Development of the IIRA: 1967-1982

In order to examine the "journey" taken by the IIRA and ILERA during the past five decades, I will focus mainly on the world congresses as well as some of the regional congresses which have been held since the foundation of the association. My account does not provide the same amount of detail on each congress and the important contributions of respective presidents to the development of the association. Rather, I have highlight congresses and issues with which I am more familiar. For convenience, I have divided the congresses and their link to the international body into three phases: the formative development of the IIRA from 1967 to 1982, the consolidation and maturation of the IIRA from 1983 to 1999, and reorientation and revitalization of IIRA/ILERA from 2000 to the present. I have drawn upon the excellent history of the association by Bruce Kaufman (2004) as well as my own recollection of world congresses, all but three of which I have attended since 1970.

The International Industrial Relations Association (IIRA) was founded in June 1966 when the presidents of the industrial relations research associations from the UK, US and Japan, as well as the head of the International Institute of Labour Studies (IILS), met in London and agreed to submit a draft constitution to their respective association. The initiative to form the IIRA had been taken in the early 1960s when Ben Roberts, Professor of Industrial Relations at the London School of Economics (LSE) was at the International Labour Organization (ILO) and discussed the idea with Robert Cox, Director of the IILS. They then approached a number of other leading academics in North America, Europe and elsewhere to garner support for their idea of an international association to promote "the study of industrial relations throughout the world in several academic disciplines" (Kaufman, 2004: 317).

At the first World Congress in September 1967, 23 invited papers were presented on 4 themes: bargaining and conflict, resistance and response to change, incomes policy and teaching, and research in industrial relations. Over 200 participants attended the congress from

39 countries. Ben Roberts was elected as president and Robert Cox as secretary of the IIRA. An executive board was established with representatives from eight countries. At the 1967 World Congress, the IIRA membership comprised 10 national industrial relations associations as full members, 11 institutional members and 160 individual members. By the time the second World Congress was held in Geneva in September 1970, these numbers had increased to 19, 36 and 341 respectively. The IILS at the ILO provided a secretariat for the IIRA, and signaled the strong support which the ILO provided for the establishment and operations of the IIRA from its early days.

My first involvement with the IIRA was when I attended the second World Congress held in Geneva in September 1970. I was about to commence a doctoral program at the London School of Economics (LSE) and was advised to attend the IIRA congress in order to gain a better appreciation for industrial relations, which was an entirely new academic field to me. The experiences I had at that congress, particularly the people whom I met, shaped my subsequent academic career. I am grateful for the opportunities which resulted from my involvement with IIRA, and later ILERA, during the next half century.

The 1970 congress was held at the old ILO building (which now houses the World Trade Organization (WTO)) in Geneva and was attended by more than 350 participants. It was a rather formal affair with addresses by Wilfred Jenks, the ILO Director, and established academics such as John Dunlop from the USA and Ben Roberts from the LSE. The sessions were held in large lecture theaters with little interaction or discussion. The program was dominated by academics from Europe and North America with few participants from other regions of the world and only a small number of students. However, the congress opened my eyes to an exciting new field (to me) of industrial relations and the ILO.

Three years later, in 1973, the third World Congress of the IIRA was hosted by the LSE in London. Together with other graduate students, I volunteered to assist with various administrative tasks and so felt more engaged in the activities of the congress. Being held at a university, rather than at the ILO, enabled the congress to be less formal and involve more students. However, compared with the 1970 congress, attendance was a little less, with around 300 participants. The main issues discussed at this time were collective bargaining, economic policies to control rising wages and prices, the high level of industrial disputes as well as concerns about rising unemployment in many countries. The focus was mainly on Europe and North America with little attention to emerging economies of Asia, Latin America and elsewhere. Issues such as gender inequality, migration and racial discrimination were not yet on the agenda of the congress.

The fourth World Congress, held in Geneva in 1976, marked the tenth anniversary of the association. John Dunlop of Harvard University (and also US Secretary for Labour) served as president from 1973-1976. In 1976, individual members numbered almost 400 from over 50 countries. The Association was still dominated by the Anglo-American countries, which contributed over half the membership, although an increasing proportion of members were joining from Europe as well as emerging interest in Asia and Latin America. The World Congress in 1979 was held at the University of Paris with Daniel Reynaud as president. The congress attracted a growing number of European attendees but there was dissatisfaction with the formal nature of the congress.

Commenting on the topics discussed at the world congresses during the 1970s, Kaufman (2004: 328) noted that "the IIRA clearly leaned toward an institutional and political economy 'externalist' perspective on labour and employment issues and de-emphasized a psychological and management 'internalist' perspective." The themes of collective bargaining, industrial disputes, the emerging problems of inflation, union and employer relations reflected the industrial relations issues of the period. The focus of the IIRA was also influenced by the "founding fathers" such as Ben Roberts from the LSE in the UK and several notable US scholars such as Gerald Somers from the University of Wisconsin, Arthur Ross at the University of California, Berkeley and John Dunlop of Harvard, all of whom were essentially institutional economists with an interest in labour relations. The founders of the Association were also concerned about establishing the legitimacy of industrial relations as an interdisciplinary field of knowledge and practice. As Roberts noted in his Presidential address of 1970, while industrial relations had been long established in some major universities, particularly in the US, "in many others, it has only recently been accepted as a branch of learning in its own right" (Kaufman, 2004: 323).

Consolidation and Maturation of the IIRA: 1983-1999

The World Congress in 1983 in Japan, hosted by President Mikio Sumiya, was the first to be held in an Asian country. The Japanese were among the founding countries of the IIRA, through the Japan Institute of Labour, a government-funded research institute. The Japanese government was enthusiastic about promoting the Japanese approach to labour-management issues even though industrial relations was not an established academic field in Japan. A pre-congress meeting was held in Tokyo to provide information on the Japanese enterprise approach to labour relations and was followed by the main congress in Kyoto. This was the first time that industry visits were arranged before the congress and many participants took advantage of the opportunity to see something of Japanese industry first-hand. Some informal meetings were also arranged alongside the proceedings of the congress to enable congress participants to engage in research discussions.

Subsequent world congresses during this decade were held in Hamburg, (then) West Germany in 1986, hosted by President Friedrich Furstenberg, and Brussels, Belgium in 1989, by President Roger Blanpain. These congresses reflected growing interest and participation by Europeans in industrial relations. The introduction of study groups on particular issues of interest also led to greater interaction between members during and between congresses and led to a number of publications based on their work. Regional congresses also began during the 1980s with the first being held in Austria in 1984. Israel hosted a regional congress in 1987 as did Singapore during the same year. During 1988, the first regional congress of the Americas was held in Canada as well as the first African regional congress in Nigeria. By the end of the 1980s, the IIRA had extended its activities to a regional level.

The issues of concern to industrial relations scholars began to change during the 1980s as the association became less Anglo-American and European centric. Kaufman (2004: 575) argued that the 1989 World Congress represented a "transition point" with the decline of institutions such as trade unions and collective bargaining and the rise of human resource management and other non-collective forms of employee relations.

In 1992, the first World Congress was held in the southern hemisphere in Sydney, Australia. This congress was notable for several reasons. It attracted a record number of participants with over 900 registrations. It also marked a significant increase in membership of the Association in all categories with a total of 1,269 individual members, 47 institutional members and 33 national members. While the congress included traditional themes, such as trade unions and the role of the state in industrial relations, it also introduced some new themes including: human resource management, the macro/micro interface in labour-market policy and practice, and industrial relations and political transformation. In his Presidential address to the congress, John Niland noted that "industrial relations is a precarious field of study" and speculated that "it is not being overly dramatic to wonder whether the discipline will survive much beyond the year 2000. If it does, certainly it will look quite different by then, and a change of name would be only part of the story" (Niland, 1994: 463). Although the discipline has survived, there have been major changes in industrial relations as an academic field of study, as predicted by Niland. Furthermore, the challenges to the discipline outlined by Niland are still relevant, that is: to remain intellectually satisfying to scholars while also being relevant and useful to both policy making and professional practice.

The 1992 World Congress was also notable for the fact that half of the papers were written by scholars from outside the Anglo-American countries. It was also the last congress from which most of the papers were published in a book, edited by Niland, Lansbury and Verevis (1994). The book included a number of authors from Asia: Japan, South Korea, Hong Kong and Singapore; as well as from both Western and Eastern Europe, Israel, South Africa and Australia. In their introduction to the volume, Lansbury and Verevis (1994) noted that while the level of unionization and collective bargaining was declining in many of the older industrialized countries, in some of the newly industrialized countries unionization was growing but taking somewhat different forms from Western traditions. They also discussed whether long-established systems of industrial relations would be so radically transformed that they will have little in common with the past (Lansbury and Verevis, 1994: 3-13).

The 1995 World Congress in Washington DC was the first to be held in the US despite the fact that John Dunlop was the second president (1973-1976) and that the US was a founding member of the Association. This congress not only continued to focus on the challenge of human resource management to industrial relations, on a global scale, but also introduced new themes such as emerging models of worker participation, new methods of negotiation, dispute resolution and joint problem solving. The congress was well attended with almost 1,000 participants and a large number of papers. As president of the Association (1992-1995). Tom Kochan initiated a series of international studies of the changing nature of industrial relations in both the industrialized and newly industrializing economies which were released at the time of the congress (Locke et al., 1995; Verma et al., 1995). These studies were followed by others which examined changes in various industries at the international level.

The final World Congress during the 1990s was held in Bologna, Italy, in 1998. Not surprisingly, this congress focused a great deal on issues of concern in Europe, including: social dialogue and democratic development, international trade agreements and social clauses, training policies and jobs as well as industrial relations in a wider social context, including the quality of work and social life. The President of the IIRA, Tiziano Treu, was the Minister for Labour in the Italian government at the time of the congress, so much of the organization was undertaken by the late Marco Biagi, then President of the Italian Industrial Relations Society. Biagi was a distinguished academic and long-term member of the international association. Tragically, in 2002, Marco Biagi was assassinated by terrorists allegedly because of his authorship of a *White Paper on the Labour*

Market in Italy: Proposals for an Active Society and Quality Employment which he undertook for the center-right government of Italy at that time.

The 1990s were marked by the growing number of IIRA study groups and the proliferation of industrial relations publications which emerged from research undertaken by these study groups. During the 1990s approximately 16 books were published by authors associated with study groups on a diverse range of topics. These included works on public service ER in Europe, employee participation through works councils, human resource policies and competitive strategies, industrial relations theory, workplace justice, labour-market discrimination and researching the world of work (see Kaufman, 2004: 570).

IIRA Becomes ILERA: Reorientation and Revitalization from 2000-2018

As befitting the beginning of the "Asian century," the World Congress in 2000 was held in Tokyo, Japan hosted by President Tadashi Hanami. The program, not surprisingly, focused on challenges facing work and labour in Asia at it entered the twenty-first century, as well as new approaches to work in the future. The congress was attended by more than 1,000 participants. Three years later, the World Congress returned to Europe with President Manfred Weiss hosting the event in Berlin, Germany. One of the key themes explored in the congress was "European integration: convergence or diversity?" The congress also posed the question in another theme: "Collective actors in industrial relations: what future?" It also examined the impact of globalization, which was just emerging as an important issue for discussion, on national and regional systems of industrial relations and ER.

In 2006, the first World Congress in Latin America, was held in

Lima, Peru. It was hosted by President Luis Aparicio Valdez who unfortunately was prevented by illness from attending. The congress attracted a record number of Latin American participants and focused on issues of concern to emerging economies. The congress stimulated growing interest in industrial relations and associated issues in Latin America. It was preceded by a regional congress in Santiago, Chile and was followed by regional congresses in São Paulo, Brazil and Buenos Aires, Argentina. ILERA played an important role in bringing academics and practitioners in industrial relations together to discuss issues of mutual interest and to observe how other countries in Latin America were handling difficult industrial relations issues.

In 2007, the European regional congress was held in Manchester, which was the first time that the international association had met in England since 1973. A major forum was held at the congress to discuss a proposal to change the name of the International Industrial Relations Association (IIRA) to the International Labour and Employment Association (ILERA). Leading the debate from opposing sides were two former presidents who had different views on this proposal. The main concern expressed by those opposing the change of name was that it would result in a move away from the association's traditional focus on industrial relations issues, such as collective bargaining and freedom of association, to a more management-oriented agenda, including human resource management. However, the decision to adopt the name International Labour and Employment Relations (ILERA) has not resulted in a decline of interest in industrial relations, but has coincided with the emergence of a broader range of labour and ER issues of concern to employers, employees, unions, governments and non-government organizations.

In 2009, Australia once again hosted the World Congress in Sydney. Almost 1,000 participants attended the congress, of whom approximately half were from outside Australia. The congress was opened by Julia Gillard, the Australian Minister for Industrial Relations who later became Prime Minister. The congress coincided with the global recession and included a major forum on the impact of the economic crisis on ER around the world. Business leaders, trade union officials and key international experts spoke at the forum. Several new themes were introduced in the congress including the changing nature of work and its future. There was a strong emphasis on workshops which were initiated by groups of participants on a wide of topics.

The Sydney Congress also offered an opportunity to review the extensive reforms of industrial relations which had been introduced under the Fair Work Act by the Labour government in Australia. This Act sought to restore the role of unions in collective bargaining and strengthen the powers of the industrial relations tribunal, after the previous conservative coalition government had radically transformed the legal foundations of the Australian system. Like many other countries represented at the congress, the system of industrial relations in Australia was undergoing fundamental changes which challenged the academic discipline to remain relevant.

The US hosted the World Congress in Philadelphia in 2012 under the leadership of President Janice Bellace. This congress was notable for the inclusion of China as a member of ILERA for the first time and a forum conducted on Chinese industrial relations. The decision by the Chinese to join ILERA was the result of a long diplomatic process which was finally brought to a successful conclusion by President Bellace. The congress also highlighted the growing of importance of industrial relations in emerging economies such as China, South Korea, Brazil and South Africa which were strongly represented in Philadelphia. By contrast, the decline in trade union coverage in many Western economies, such as the US, were highlighted at the congress and considerable debate occurred about whether this trend will continue or be reversed.

In 2015, the first World Congress was held in Africa, although several regional congresses had been successfully conducted on the continent in previous years. Evance Kalula was the first African to be elected as president of ILERA. The congress attracted a record number of African participants and highlighted both the problems and potential which exist for the development of industrial relations and the improvement in working conditions and wages of Africans. The congress emphasized the need to take a much broader view of how industrial relations could assist both social and economic development in emerging nations and the role which South Africa could play in improving working conditions in the region.

One of the most encouraging developments within the ILERA in recent years is the number of regional congresses which have been held in Asia, Latin America and Africa. The most recent Asian regional congress was hosted in Beijing by the Chinese national affiliate of ILERA. Even though most of the individual members of ILERA are still drawn from Europe and North America, many national associations have been formed in other regions of the world. Included among the many challenges facing ILERA, however, are how to expand membership in regions such as Asia where major growth in population and economic development is occurring. In most Asian countries, the right to join unions and engage in collective bargaining is very limited and industrial relations has only a minor presence as an academic field. It remains to be seen whether the decline in labour and ER as a field of study in its traditional heartland of the US and the UK will be reversed. These are major challenges for the future of ILERA.

Labour and Employment Relations in an Era of Globalization

There are a number of reasons why ILERA will continue to have an important role to play in the academic field and practical application of ER. Changes in the world economy, that are commonly referred to as globalization, have had significant consequences for work and ER but have also provided the opportunity to reassert the relevance of the discipline in understanding the impact of these changes on the nature of work, people and organizations. Globalization has been defined as "a process of rapid integration between countries … driven by the liberalization of international trade and by freer capital flows" (Torres, 2001: 8). Globalization has exerted pressures on job security in a number of countries as workers have been displaced by shifts in the competitive position of enterprises in world markets and the position of countries in the international division of labour.

There are competing views about the effects of globalization on the labour market. Some analysts argue that globalization produces convergence in labour standards across countries and regions, while others suggest that the pressures associated with globalization are refracted through national-level institutional arrangements, resulting in continued diversity (see Katz and Darbishire, 2000). Clearly, however, the impact of globalization on ER is an important recent development and there is a need to take into account the influence of international economic forces as well as the role of nation states and their institutions in shaping labour markets, as well as economic and social outcomes.

Although multinational corporations (MNCs) have existed for many decades, their influence has increased with the growth in foreign direct investment (FDI) and the growing "interconnectedness" of the world economy. As noted by Wedderburn (2007), in relation to the impact on labour law, "what we underrated was … the power of emergent globalised capital." According to UNCTAD (2005: xix), the number of MNCs has grown exponentially over the past three decades. MNCs currently account for about two-thirds of world exports of goods and services, of which a significant share is intra-firm trade. This form of trade is less subject to external market prices and is determined by internal decisions of the MNCs.

As the production networks of MNCs have become more complex, involving multiple tiers of suppliers around the world (such as the auto industry), it has become more difficult to determine where decisions on work and ER are made (Dicken, 2007). The internationalization of production organization and supply chains, together with the liberalization of cross-national capital flows, has made it increasingly difficult to identify the owners of productive assets and companies as employers of labour. As noted by White (2004): "shareholding, as the dominant form of ownership has turned into a jungle of equity ownership relations in funds and funds of funds, making it virtually impossible to know what is owned by whom."

The ability of trade unions, at the national and industry level, to negotiate effectively with MNCs has become increasingly limited. Globalization was described by the International Confederation of Free Trade Unions as "the greatest challenge facing trade unions" (Kyloh, 1998). In response, trade unions have adopted a multi-level strategy, with varied success. At the national level, many unions have been devoting resources to recruitment and organizing, providing additional services to members, and joining forces with NGOs and community groups in particular campaigns. At regional and international levels, unions have established information networks about bargaining practices and agreements reached with MNCs in an effort to coordinate bargaining. In some industries, such as clothing and textiles, unions have been able to achieve agreements with employers on codes of conduct and social labeling which are aimed at getting employers to adopt acceptable labour practices and abide by international employment standards established by the ILO. Recently, some global union federations have been successful at negotiating international framework agreements with MNCs, but these are still a few in number and at an early stage of development (Papadakis, 2008).

While globalization has become the focus of attention in recent years, there is ample evidence that national and, in some cases, sub-national factors continue to play an important role in structuring relationships between employers and employees. Thelen's work on Germany provides a good example of this phenomenon as she demonstrates that despite the pressures associated with globalization, distinctive features of German industrial relations, notably the two-tier system of employee representation, have prevented the wholesale deregulation of the German labour market. Indeed, Thelen has argued that the increased competitive pressures associated with globalization have encouraged German employers to renew their commitment to aspects of employee representation at the enterprise level and to industry-wide bargaining (Thelen, 2000; Thelen and Kume, 2003). However, more recently, Thelen (2014) has noted that service-sector employers in Germany have favored more "flexible" employment arrangements compared with those in manufacturing.

There is also literature which rejects the notion that globalization creates irresistible pressures for convergence of capitalist economies on a neoliberal model. Most notable is the "varieties of capitalism" (VoC) approach advocated by Hall and Soskice (2001) among others. They argue that it is possible to identify at least two institutional equilibria which resolve the coordination problems associated with a market economy. First, "liberal market economies" (LMEs) rely on markets and hierarchies to resolve coordination problems and the United States is the prime example. Second, "coordinated market economies" (CMEs) use greater non-market mechanisms to resolve coordination problems internally and externally. Germany is the prime exemplar of CMEs but other northern European countries also fit this category. The VoC approach highlights the causal significance of national-level institutions in shaping national responses to international pressures. While increased competition associated with globalization (and individualization) of bargaining in LMEs, this does not necessarily follow in CMEs.

Among the criticisms of the VoC approach is that it does not contain enough variety and focuses only on those countries to which the model can be applied (Allen, 2004). Not only are there other European countries which do not fit easily into either the LME or CME categories (see Hancke et al., 2007) but some Asian countries such as Japan, Korea and China appear to combine elements of both categories. Furthermore, systems of multi-level governance such as the European Union pose significant challenges to the nationally bounded and distinct description of institutions on which the VoC approach is based. Deeg and Jackson (2007) argue that the increasingly international character of institutional actors, notably capital, means that the national-level institutions create less constraints than depicted by the VoC approach.

Wailes (2008) has argued that it is necessary to rethink the relationship between the international and the national when seeking to understand current developments in industrial relations, especially in order to include the effects of a regional dimension such as the European Union. He notes that literature on ER practices in MNCs provides a concrete example of how this form of institutional incompleteness can affect national patterns of industrial relations. Almond and Tempel (2006) demonstrated that while the institutional context of host nations and the power relations within MNCs help shape the ER practices across their subsidiaries, MNCs also exhibit a strong "country of origin" effect. This supports an earlier research by Ferner (1997) which found that the tendency for MNCs to diffuse key employment practices across their subsidiaries reflected the extent to which MNCs and their management were embedded in the institutional context of their home countries. Wailes (2008) cites criticisms of the institutional approach in comparative capitalism to how the concept of institutional incompleteness can be used to bring international and European-level developments into the analysis of industrial relations while at the same time remaining attentive to the enduring and significant role played by national-level arrangements.

A Multi-Level Institutional Perspective on Labour and Employment Relations

Research by Wright et al. (2017) identify three institutional spheres of labour and ER and their modes of interaction which may assist in identifying the impact of changes when analyzing and comparing different countries: the national, the sectoral and transnational, as shown in Figure 8.1.

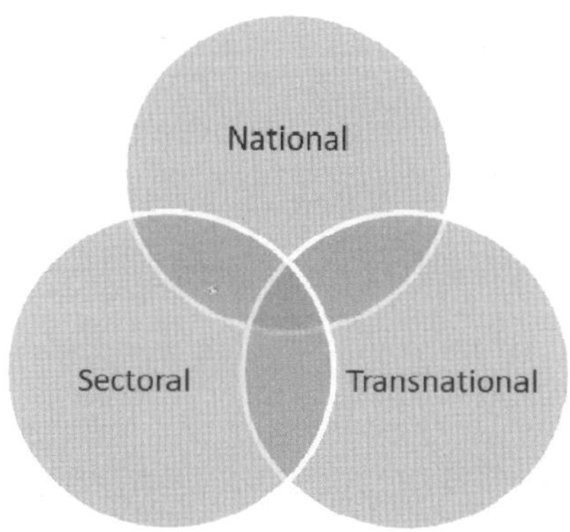

Figure 8.1 Institutional spheres influencing labour and employment relations arrangements

National Institutions

Although some argue that globalization has led to a decline in the importance of the national state in relation to labour and ER, national institutions continue to play an important role in influencing the strategic choices of employers, unions, policy-makers and other ER actors. Distinct national "models" have been identified in certain countries, which ER actors in other countries have sought to emulate or avoid. One example is the Danish system of "flexicurity," which has been seen as a potential model for other economies (Madsen et al., 2016).

A national system helps to explain similarities and differences in employer preferences and employment regulation of, among other things, the gendered nature of labour markets, employee participation, job quality, vocational training systems and links between labour markets and immigration policies, collective bargaining and union membership density (see Frege and Godard, 2014; Frege and Kelly, 2004; Lansbury and Wailes, 2008; Goergen et al., 2012; Wright, 2016). National institutions still matter, and have a continuing impact on strategic choices of ER actors including: the form of employment, the determination of pay and other working conditions, and how their interests are represented.

However, changes in how labour and ER arrangements are coordinated suggest that the utility of national systems approach is diminishing. There is still much cooperation among employers in CMEs such as Denmark and in the German manufacturing sector about pay determination and skill formation. However, in Germany the private-services sector and small- and medium-sized enterprises have opted out of sectoral bargaining in favor of enterprise-based determination typically without unions (Keller and Kirsch, 2016; Madsen et al., 2016). Lifetime employment, traditionally a hallmark of the Japanese system, has come under pressure from changing patterns of corporate governance that have adopted shareholder-driven models to a greater extent than hitherto. This has led to a growth in non-standard and precarious employment (Suzuki et al., 2016). Similar outcomes can be seen in South Korea (Lee, 2016).

Sectoral Institutions

Thelen (2014) argues that a significant limitation of the VoC approach relates to its extrapolation of the specific preferences of manufacturing employers to be the coordination preferences of all employers. The structural shift from manufacturing to services that has occurred in nearly all developed economies "has upset previous political dynamics because both firms and workers in these emerging sectors have interests that are very different from their counterparts in traditional manufacturing," according to Thelen (2014: 25). Manufacturing employers tend to prefer CME-type arrangements, such as long-term employment relationships and skill regimes focused on the development of enterprise and industry-specific skills. In contrast, service-sector employers tend to favor general and portable skill regimes and arrangements that facilitate more "flexible" employment relationships (see also Batt et al., 2009; Bechter et al., 2012; Caviedes, 2010; Katz and Darbishire, 2000).

In some countries, shifts in the sectoral composition of the national labour market have had an influence on the dominant preferences of employers. In Australia, for example, there has been a move away from non-market coordination of skill formation and pay determination, which until relatively recently were favored by manufacturing employers. However, reflecting their relative decline, the influence of manufacturing employers over national ER regulation has waned. By contrast, there is a preference for labour-market deregulation among employers in the private-services and resource sectors, which have both experienced much growth in the twenty-first century. This shift in the dominant employer coordination preferences has served to embed the "liberal" market (LME) features of Australia's ER system (Wright and Lansbury, 2014).

In Germany, while the long-standing preferences for non-market coordination continues among manufacturing, finance and public-sector employers, as mentioned above, market coordination preferences are becoming increasingly evident among private-services sector and small-business employers. The growth in private-service-sector employment is arguably producing a transformational shift in the post-1945 "German model" of ER (Bechter et al., 2012; Hassel, 2014). More generally, this trend illustrates the extent to which sectoral issues, such as the mix of industries in a particular national economy, can impact the strategic choices of ER actors independently of national-level institutional arrangements.

Sector-based logics, then, may cut across national systems, thus enabling increased diversity in ER arrangements within countries (Marginson and Sisson, 2004). Without discounting the influence of national systems, the role of sector-level variables - such as pay determination and skill formation arrangements, technology, the organization of production and product market regulations - should be given greater weight as a potential influence of strategic choice (Bechter et al., 2012; Katz and Darbishire, 2000).

Transnational Institutions

The growth of multilateral forms of governance over the past decade or so indicates that the influence of transnational factors on actors' strategic choices needs to be included more comprehensively in international and comparative ER analysis (Meardi and Marginson, 2014).

"Private" forms of transnational governance, such as the commercial policies and practices of MNCs, are also increasingly important for understanding the strategic choices of ER actors (Katz and Wailes, 2014). MNCs have extended their commercial presence and power by creating subsidiaries offshore and through global production networks that engage suppliers located in other countries, in many cases enabling MNCs to reduce labour costs (Lakhani et al., 2013; Locke et al., 2013; Wright and Kaine, 2015). For example, many US enterprises have offshored parts of their activities to emerging economies (Katz and Colvin, 2016). Japanese manufacturers have created many jobs in offshore subsidiaries (Suzuki et al., 2016). In China, employment agencies engaging low-paid workers have benefited from widespread downsizing among state-owned enterprises and of significant migration of workers from rural to urban areas (Cooke, 2016).

In Denmark, the EU Posted Workers Directive to an extent has enabled employers to circumvent collective agreements by hiring workers through subcontractors registered in Central and Eastern European countries with lower pay levels (Madsen et al., 2016), thereby allowing employers to gain similar cost advantages that might otherwise have been achieved through offshoring. Outsourcing and offshoring often entail a shift to more market-oriented relationships between a lead enterprise and a supplier enterprise governed by commercial imperatives (see Gereffi et al., 2005; Marchington et al., 2004; Wright, 2016). Therefore, even in CMEs, increased use of outsourcing and offshoring has produced more "market" ER arrangements.

Lastly, various international institutions can directly influence the strategic choices of ER actors. For example, the conventions of the International Labour Organization (ILO) are reflected in the laws of countries that ratify them (ILO, 2008). It is also increasingly common for ILO conventions to serve as benchmarks for voluntary instruments relating to ER arrangements of offshore suppliers and subsidiaries, such as MNC codes of conduct and global framework agreements between global union federations and MNEs (Ryder, 2015). These transnational instruments have helped partly to address the problem of weak regulation of labour standards in global production networks (Ruggie, 2013). Nevertheless, national institutions and/or sectoral institutions also influence the impact of such transnational instruments on local ER arrangements (Locke et al., 2013).

Intersections Between Different Spheres of Labour and Employment Relations

It has been noted how the role of institutions at the national, sectoral and transnational levels influence labour and employment arrangements. These institutions may have a more dominant impact in certain scenarios and may operate relatively discretely from institutions operating at other scales. For instance, the systems of "awards" which influence workplace pay determination in Australia or flexicurity which influence employer decisions relating to hiring and firing in Denmark might be seen primarily as national ER institutions that transnational and sectoral institutions have played a little role in creating and sustaining. Other strategic choices might be a product of a combination of two institutional spheres, but not the third. For example, Appelbaum et al. (2010) explored the interplay between national regulation and sectoral characteristics in their study of low-paid work in six developed economies, finding that sectoral characteristics appeared to be more important than national regulatory frameworks for understanding ER arrangements in the hotel industry. However, this was not the case in some other industries, such as retailing, where the influence of national institutions was much stronger. In other cases, national, sectoral and transnational institutions may all impact ER processes or outcomes. For instance, the nature of work organization in the automotive industry is influenced by the preferences of MNCs who own the production plants, sectoral norms regarding production techniques, and factors pertaining to local ER including skill-development arrangements, labour costs, the organization of labour, and employment laws and regulations (Wailes et al., 2008). There is considerable scope for future research for examining the different ways that distinct institutional spheres intersect to influence work and ER arrangements.

Conclusion

Labour and ER as a field of knowledge, and ILERA as an institution which encourages research, face a number of enduring and accelerating challenges in the context of changes to the "stable state" which existed for many years when unionization rates were relatively high across the developed market economies and collective bargaining was well-established in key industries, such as manufacturing, and in the public sector (see Arrowsmith and Pulignano, 2013). As union membership has fallen, bargaining coverage has declined and there has been a replacement of collective labour-management relations with more individualized forms of employment contracts. Labour markets have been progressively deregulated in many economies and the proportion of the workforce undertaking contingent forms of work on non-standard employment contracts has grown. Laws have become more restrictive in relation to collective action such as strikes and the number of formal industrial disputes has declined. This has meant that labour and ER, if it remains too narrowly focused on collective bargaining and industrial conflict, will continue to be a less popular field of study, even though issues related to worklife have become increasingly important to economic and social progress.

While the regulation of the workplace and interaction between employers and unions remain key concerns to the field of labour and ER, other issues related to people at work, employment, and organizations are important in bringing a broader perspective to the subject. Hence, labour and ER need to maintain a multidisciplinary approach to issues of work and the employment relationship and to connect micro-level issues at the workplace level with macro-level issues in society and the economy. It needs to combine its concern for the traditional social partners - unions, employer associations and the state - with newer actors such as non-governmental organization (NGO) and community organizations which are actively concerned with issues at work and in the workplace. The expertise which labour and ER scholars and practitioners have developed in dispute resolution between unions and employers can be applied to other areas of conflict in the workplace. Alternative methods of providing a voice and influence for employees at their place of work should be a natural province of work and ER specialists.

While the national or sub-national level will remain the focus of labour and ER in most countries, new developments at the regional and international levels will require a multi-level approach to the subject. Globalization of the economy means that labour and ER will continue to interact with issues of international trade. International organizations, such as the ILO, WTO and World Bank have an opportunity to play an increasingly significant role along with international employers' groups, global union federations and a growing variety of NGOs. However, MNCs are likely to be the locus of employment for growing numbers of people and will exert considerable influence on the future of ER.

While labour and ER in developed economies will continue to blend continuity with change, newly industrializing economies in Asia and elsewhere will develop their own approaches and work-related institutions which reflect their own traditions and needs. However, as argued by other notable scholars, such as Budd (2004) and Edwards (2007), if the field of labour and ER is to remain relevant to the social and economic justice of people at work as well as contribute to improving both business and public policies around the world, it must maintain its long-held concern to achieve a balance between equity and efficiency in relation to people at work.

Acknowledgment

I wish to thank my colleagues Greg Bamber, Nick Wailes and Chris F. Wright, for allowing me to utilize material from our jointly authored work (Bamber et al., 2016) which has been incorporated into this chapter, and to Jim Arrowsmith for his valuable advice on an earlier version of this chapter.

References

Allen, M. (2004) "The Varieties of Capitalism Paradigm: Not Enough Variety?," *Socio-Economic Review*, 2(1): 87-108.

Almond, P. and Tempel A. (2006) "Multinationals and National Business Systems: A Power and Institutions Perspective," in Almond, P. and Ferner, A. (eds.), *American Multinationals in Europe: Managing Employment Relations across National Borders*, Oxford University Press.

Appelbaum, E., Bosch, G., Gautié, J., Mason, G., Mayhew, K., Salverda, W., Schmitt, J. and Westergaard-Nielsen, N. (2010) "Introduction and Overview," in Gautié, J. and Schmitt, J. (eds.), *Low-Wage*

Work in the Wealthy World, Russell Sage, pp. 1-32.

Arrowsmith, J. and Pulignano, V. (eds.), (2013) *The Transformation of Employment Relations in Europe: Institutions and Outcomes in the Age of Globalization*, Routledge.

Bamber, G.J., Lansbury, R.D., Wailes, N. and Wright, C.F. (eds.), (2016) *International and Comparative Employment Relations: National Regulation, Global Changes* (6th edition), Allen and Unwin/ Sage Publications.

Batt, R., Holman, D. and Holtgrewe, U. (2009) "The Globalization of Service Work: Comparative Institutional Perspectives on Call Centers," *Industrial and Labour Relations Review*, 62(4), pp. 453-488.

Bechter, B., Brandl, B. and Meardi, G. (2012) "Sectors or Countries? Typologies and Levels of Analysis in Comparative Industrial Relations," *European Journal of Industrial Relations*, 18(3), pp. 185-202.

Budd, J. (2004) *Employment with a Human Face: Balancing Efficiency, Equity and Voice*, Cornell University Press.

Caviedes, A.A. (2010) *Prying Open Fortress Europe: The Turn to Sectoral Labour Migration*, Lexington Books.

Cooke, F.L. (2016) "Employment Relations in China," in Bamber, G.J, Lansbury, R.D, Wailes, N. and Wright, C.F. (eds.), *International and Comparative Employment Relations: National Regulation, Global Changes* (6th edition), Sage, pp. 291-315.

Deeg, R. and Jackson, G. (2007) "Towards a More Dynamic Theory of Capitalist Variety," *Socio-Economic Review*, 5(1), pp. 149-179.

Dicken, P. (2007) *Global Shift: Mapping the Changing Contours of the World Economy*, Sage.

Edwards, P. (2007) *Justice in the Workplace: Why it is Important and Why a New Public Policy Initiative is Needed*, The Work Foundation.

Ferner, A. (1997) "Country of Origins Effects and HRM in Multinational Companies," *Human Resource Management Journal*, 7(1), pp. 201-217.

Frege, C. and Godard, J. (2014) "Varieties of Capitalism and Job Quality: The Attainment of Civic Principles at Work in the United States and Germany," *American Sociological Review*, 79(5), pp. 942-965.

Frege, C. and Kelly, J. (eds.), (2004) *Varieties of Unionism: Strategies for Union Revitalisation in a Globalising Economy*, Oxford University Press.

Gereffi, G., Humphrey, J. and Sturgeon, T. (2005) "The Governance of Global Value Chains," *Review of International Political Economy*, 12(1), pp. 78-104.

Goergen, M., Brewster, C., Wood, G. and Wilkinson, A. (2012) "Varieties of Capitalism and Investments in Human Capital," *Industrial Relations*, 51(s1), pp. 501-527.

Hall, P.A. and Soskice, D. (eds.), (2001) *Varieties of Capitalism: The Institutional Foundations of Comparative Advantage*, Oxford University Press.

Hancke, B., Rhodes, M. and Thatcher, M. (2007) "Introduction: Beyond Varieties of Capitalism," in Hancke, B., Rhodes, M. and Thatcher, M. (eds.), *Beyond Varieties of Capitalism: Conflict, Contradictions and Complementarities in the European Economy*, Oxford University Press, pp. 3-38.

Hassel, A. (2014) "The Paradox of Liberalization—Understanding Dualism and the Recovery of the German Political Economy," *British Journal of Industrial Relations*, 52(1), pp. 57-81.

International Labour Organization (ILO) (2008) "From Better Factories to Better Work," *World of Work: The Magazine of the ILO*, 62, pp. 10-13.

Katz, H.C. and Colvin, A.J.S. (2016) "Employment Relations in the United States," in Bamber, G.J, Lansbury, R.D., Wailes, N. and Wright, C.F. (eds.), *International and Comparative Employment Relations: National Regulation, Global Changes* (6th edition), Sage Publications.

Katz, H.C. and Darbishire, O. (2000) *Converging Divergences: Worldwide Changes in Employment Systems*, Cornell University Press.

Katz, H.C. and Wailes, N. (2014) "Convergence and Divergence in Employment Relations," in Wilkinson, A., Wood, G. and Deeg, R. (eds.), *The Oxford Handbook of Employment Relations: Comparative Employment Systems*, Oxford University Press, pp. 42-61.

Kaufman, B. (2004) *The Global Evolution of Industrial Relations: Events, Ideas and the IIRA*, International Labour Office.

Keller, B.K. and Kirsch, A. (2016) "Employment Relations in Germany," in Bamber, G.J., Lansbury, R.D., Wailes, N. and Wright, C.F. (eds.), *International and Comparative Employment Relations: National Regulation, Global Changes* (6th edition), Sage Publications.

Kyloh, R. (ed.), (1998) *Mastering the Challenge of Globalisation: Towards a Trade Union Agenda*, International Labour Organization.

Lakhani, T., Kuruvilla, S. and Avgar, A. (2013) "From the Firm to the Network: Global Value Chains and Employment Relations Theory," *British Journal of Industrial Relations*, 51(3) pp. 440-472.

Lansbury, R.D. and Verevis, C. (eds.), (1994) "Change and Continuity in Industrial Relations: An Introduction," in Niland, J.R., Lansbury, R.D. and Verevis, C. (eds.), *The Future of Industrial Relations; Global Change and Challenges*, Sage Publications.

Lansbury, R.D. and Wailes, N. (2008) "Employee Involvement and Direct Participation," in Blyton, P., Bacon, N., Fiorito, J. and Heery, E. (eds.), *Sage Handbook of Industrial Relations*, Sage

Publications, pp. 434-446.

Lee, B.H. (2016) "Employment Relations in South Korea," In Bamber, G.J, Lansbury, R.D., Wailes, N. and Wright, C.F (eds.), *International and Comparative Employment Relations: National Regulation, Global Changes* (6th edition), Sage Publications.

Locke, R.M., Kochan, T.A. and Piore, M. (eds.), (1995) *Employment Relations in a Changing World Economy*, MIT Press.

Locke, R.M., Rissing, B.A. and Pal, T. (2013) "Complements or Substitutes? Private Codes, State Regulation and the Enforcement of Labour Standards in Global Supply Chains," *British Journal of Industrial Relations*, 51(3), pp. 519-552.

Madsen, J.S., Due, J. and Andersen, S.K. (2016) "Employment Relations in Denmark," in Bamber, G.J., Lansbury, R.D., Wailes, N. and Wright, C.F. (eds.), *International and Comparative Employment Relations: National Regulation, Global Changes* (6th edition), Sage, pp. 208-236.

Marchington, M., Grimshaw, D., Rubery, J. and Willmott, H. (eds.), (2004) *Fragmenting Work: Blurring Organizational Boundaries and Disordering Hierarchies*, Oxford University Press.

Marginson, P. and Sisson, K. (with Arrowsmith, J.) (2004) *European Integration and Industrial Relations: Multi-Level Governance in the Making*, Palgrave.

Meardi, G. and Marginson, P. (2014) "Global Labour Governance: Potential and Limits of an Emerging Perspective," *Work, Employment and Society*, 28(4), pp. 651-662.

Niland, J.R. (1994) "Change and the International Exchange of Ideas," in Niland, J.R., Lansbury, R.D. and Verevis, C. (eds.), (1994) *The Future of Industrial Relations; Global Change and Challenges*, Sage Publications.

Niland J.R., Lansbury, R.D. and Verevis, C. (eds.), (1994) *The Future of*

Industrial Relations; Global Change and Challenges, Sage Publications.

Papadakis, K. (2008) "Research on Transnational Social Dialogue and International Framework Agreements," *The International Labour Review*, 147(1), pp. 100-104.

Ruggie, J.G. (2013) *Just Business: Multinational Corporations and Human Rights*, WW Norton and Company.

Ryder, G. (2015) "The International Labour Organization: The Next 100 Years," *Journal of Industrial Relations*, 57(5), pp. 748-757.

Suzuki, H., Kubo, K. and Ogura, K. (2016) "Employment Relations in Japan," in Bamber, G.J., Lansbury, R.D. Wailes, N. and Wright, C.F. (eds.), *International and Comparative Employment Relations: National Regulation, Global Changes* (6th edition), Sage Publications.

Thelen, K. (2000) "Why the German Employers Cannot Bring Themselves to Dismantle the German Model," in Iversen, T., Pontusson, J. and Soskice, D. (eds.), *Unions, Employers and Central Banks: Macro-Economic Coordination and Institutional Change in Social Market Economies*, Cambridge University Press.

Thelen, K. (2014) *Varieties of Liberalization and the New Politics of Social Solidarity*, Cambridge University Press.

Thelen, K. and Kume, I. (2003) "The Future of Nationally Embedded Capitalism: Industrial Relations in Germany and Japan," in Streeck, W. and Yamamura, K. (eds.), *The End of Diversity? Prospects for German and Japanese Capitalism*, Cornell University Press.

Torres, R. (2001) *Towards a Socially Sustainable World Economy: An Analysis of the Social Pillars of Globalization*, International Labour Organization.

United Nations Commission for Trade and Development (UNCTAD) (2005) *World Investment Report 2005: Transnational Corporations and the Internationalisation of Research and Development*, United

Nations.

Verma, A., Kochan, T.A. and Lansbury, R.D. (1995) *Employment Relations in the Growing Asian Economies*, Routledge.

Wailes, N. (2008) "Are National Industrial Relations Regimes Becoming Institutionally Incomplete?," in Rönnmar, M. (ed.), *EU Industrial Relations versus National Industrial Relations*, Wolters Kluwer, pp. 3-14.

Wailes, N., Lansbury, R.D., Kitay, J. and Kirsch, A. (2008) "Globalization, Varieties of Capitalism and Employment Relations in the Automotive Assembly Industry," in Blainpain, R. and Lansbury, R.D. (eds.), *Globalization and Employment Relations in the Auto Assembly Industry: A Study of Seven Countries*, Kluwer, pp. 1-11.

Wedderburn, Lord (2007) "Labour Law 2008: Forty Years On," *Industrial Law Journal*, 36(4), pp. 397-424.

White, S. (2004) "Markets, Time and Citizenship," *Renewal: A Journal of Labour Politics*, 12(3), pp. 50-63.

Wright, C.F. (2016) "Leveraging Reputational Risk: Sustainable Sourcing Campaigns for Improving Labour Standards in Production Networks," *Journal of Business Ethics*, 137(1), pp. 195-210.

Wright, C.F. and Kaine, S. (2015) "Supply Chains, Production Networks and the Employment Relationship," *Journal of Industrial Relations*, 57(4), pp. 483-501.

Wright, C.F., and Lansbury, R.D. (2014) "Trade Unions and Economic Reform in Australia, 1983-2013," *Singapore Economic Review*, 59(4), pp. 1-22.

Wright, C.F., Wailes, N., Bamber, G.J. and Lansbury, R.D. (2017) "Beyond National Systems: A Research Agenda for International and Comparative Employment Relations," *Employment Rights and Responsibilities Journal*, 29(4), pp. 247-257.

ILERA: Building on Tradition and Values in Responding to the Challenges of the Information Age[1]

Janice R. Bellace

09

The theme of ILERA's 16th World Congress in Philadelphia was "Beyond Borders: Governance of Work in a Global Economy." This theme still resonates today, as Manfred Weiss' contribution highlights, but in only six years, another theme has captured our attention, the implications of a digital economy. Having read several of the other past-presidents' contributions, I attempt not to repeat their excellent work, but will present what I deem to be some of the major issues that will face ILERA as the era of industrialization ends and we move fully into the Information (Digital) Age.

Before turning to that, however, I would like to discuss ILERA, as an association. When invited to contribute to this volume celebrating ILERA's 50th anniversary, I was told that my contribution could take many forms, and could include personal recollections or observations. It is most appropriate to do so on ILERA's 50th anniversary, as those deeply involved in ILERA over the years have made it what it is today.

ILERA as a Sustainable, Growing Association

For some time there has been discussion about the future of the field of industrial relations, and even of the International Labour Organization (ILO). Many pessimists point to the decline in the number of unionized firms, or lack of interest in "industrial relations" or the inability of certain entities, such as the ILO, to achieve their goals. But, as Maupain points out, these critics forward a false dilemma.[2] The important question is whether the organization's purpose is still relevant and if so, whether the organization is staying true to its purpose. As long as people work and are paid for working so they can support themselves and their families, the subjects ILERA studies will remain relevant to society. The history of ILERA demonstrates that it has stayed true to its purpose and there is no reason to doubt that this will change in future. But voluntary, international associations do face challenges that they must confront and surmount.

The Sustainability of ILERA

International academic associations historically have confronted the challenge of cohesion and sustainability. Members rarely see each other, and until recently distance made communication difficult and often expensive. Email and social media have contributed greatly to making communication easier, but there is still the difficulty of identifying who in another country might be suitable to be a committee chair, or a session organizer, or the convener of a study group. Other issues not found in national associations arise, such as judging the quality of abstract papers written by authors in foreign countries. And the style of argument and the presentation of data and findings may be so different as to present the referee with the challenge of being fair in the evaluation.

National and international associations also differ in the "tone" of the congresses. At national academic meetings, members attend for many reasons, chief among them being the desire to be informed of the latest research on certain topics. But invariably many participants attend for the networking opportunities. They find out about possible job openings elsewhere, they obtain useful and often non-public information about the terms of employment at other universities, they get "seen" and as a result may be considered for journal editorships, or committee chairs within the association. As a result, the atmosphere at major national academic associations can be somewhat intense, and interactions are often transactional.

Members attend international academic meetings for many reasons, one of which is the desire to be informed of the latest research on certain topics. But equally important is simply the desire to learn - to learn what topics interest people in other countries, how they frame certain issues, how the accepted wisdom on a given issue is different than that prevailing in one's home country. There are few, if any, networking opportunities. People talk to others at the congress because they find the persons interesting, not because they can be of use to one's career. Conversations tend to be broad ranging, as a member from one country may have to explain political and societal developments in his/her country so as to give a meaningful answer to the specific question asked. As a result, the atmosphere at a major international academic association meeting is usually somewhat relaxed, with true social interaction occurring.

All of this explains the enduring appeal of ILERA. In the early 1960s, when Ben Roberts broached the idea of a group of national academic associations coming together to form an international association for the purpose of studying industrial relations, the driving motivation was the desire to learn. The founders of ILERA were willing to venture into areas where even senior professors had little knowledge, to admit lack of expertise and to learn from the research of others.

Another major source of appeal is the multidisciplinary nature of ILERA congresses. Today it is fashionable to talk about interdisciplinary or multidisciplinary work, but most associations are solidly discipline based. Some national associations that are members of ILERA have most of their members from one discipline, for instance, from labour economics, or law or sociology or political science. In contrast, ILERA has persons from all these disciplines coming together to discuss one topic. It can provide a lively, if confusing discussion on a topic, for instance, gender pay equity, as labour economists will discuss how labour markets determine wages, psychologists may consider notions of value, and lawyers might debate the meaning of equal in a statutory guarantee of equal pay. The appealing part is that an ILERA participant, steeped in one discipline and perhaps quite uninformed about another, can hear how that discipline approaches the same phenomenon, and can ask questions without fear of being branded ignorant.

In this quest to learn from others, ILERA provides another opportunity. Most associations have one type of member, for instance, academics or practitioners. Anyone who attends the meetings of academic associations can sympathize with the reaction of practitioners that the policies proposed by many academics simply have no connection with the real world. ILERA is different. Although ILERA was started by academics, most came from a national association that included practitioners also, admittedly practitioners with an interest in research findings and policy. Sometimes this mixing can create tension, but overall, for ILERA it has provided much richer, robust discussions. For academics, this opportunity to listen to and understand the needs and concerns of practitioners, be they ministry staff or private practitioners, not only illuminates the complexity of an issue but points to the bounds of potential solutions. Practitioners, especially in the private sector, have sometimes provided an early warning system of impending changes, as they are on the front line confronting competition in industry. This has been especially true with regard to the impact of globalization on employment and on national industrial relations systems.

These factors explain the appeal of ILERA. But a critical element of its sustainability is the ILO, which over the past 50 years, has been willing to act as the secretariat, an invaluable resource for a far-flung membership. Often the role of the ILO is hidden, as if behind a screen, and in front is ILERA's Secretary (serving as the executive director), who has always been an ILO official. It is known that the Secretary is in Geneva and serves both as an operations manager and an adviser to the president. Persons such as Alan Gladstone, Tayo Fashoyin and Giuseppe Casale have provided crucial support and guidance to ILERA. The Secretary also has an assistant and that person is the keeper of the files, and in today's world, the person who maintains the website, a vital source of information and communication. But more than that, the ILO has acted to further links among scholars and practitioners around the world, has supported congresses, has assisted with certain publications, has provided information on labour relations and labour law developments, and has identified opportunities for broadening ILERA's membership. In this regard, the ILO connection has been particularly helpful in the last ten years in facilitating China's joining ILERA, and in supporting the emergence of a southern Africa regional group meeting under the auspices of ILERA.

From IIRA to ILERA

In 1967, when the new international association was founded, the four founding institutions selected as the new name, the International

Industrial Relations Association, relying on the term two of them used. The Americans had long called the field "industrial relations" and the US affiliate, founded in 1947, was called the Industrial Relations Research Association. The British had formed the Inter-University Study Group in Industrial Relations in 1950.[3] In contrast, the two other founding members focused on "labour" with the Japanese member called the Japan Institute of Labour, and there was the International Institute for Labour Studies. There appears not to have been any discussion at the time about whether "industrial relations" connoted something broader or narrower than "labour studies."

The term "industrial relations" was not widely used around the world. As Kaufman has noted, the term was first used in the US in the first part of the twentieth century, and by 1912 it was so accepted that the US government committee appointed by President Taft to study labour problems and to make recommendations was called the "U.S. Commission on Industrial Relations."[4] The label stemmed from management's perspective that they had a problem with their workers in their factories.[5] At the hearings of the US Commission on Industrial Relations, John D. Rockefeller, Jr. testified and admitted that there were problems in the relations with workers in the coal industry and indicated that improvements in relations could be made by management. By the 1920s, courses in industrial relations were appearing at university level, most notably at the University of Wisconsin where John R. Commons taught.

The term "industrial relations" did not translate well. A literal translation produced a meaningless label in many languages. Even a description of the issues covered did not always align with the situation as seen by scholars and policy makers in other countries. Similarly, concepts like "industrial democracy," advanced by Sidney and Beatrice Webb, gained no traction in the US. But by the late 1940s, the widespread use of the term "industrial relations" in the United States was established, and major universities, such as Cornell and UCLA, started schools of industrial and labour relations. With younger scholars from Britain and Europe, such as Ben Roberts, Friedrich Furstenberg, Roger Blanpain and Tiziano Treu, spending time in the US on study programs in the 1950s and early 1960s, the American term was exported to the European continent. These future presidents of ILERA may not have been able to give a precise definition of "industrial relations" but they understood what topics the term covered. Thus, in 1967, the appellation "industrial relations" was the only serious candidate for the title of the new international association. The adoption of this name in itself was influential, for associations and academic groups in non-Anglophone countries began to use the label "industrial relations," even though the term was unknown and confusing in their own language, in part because of the IIRA and in part because they could understand from John Dunlop's formulation in *Industrial Relations Systems*[6] that the conceptual ground covered was one that interested them.[7]

But over the years, a problem with the name emerged. The difficulty was that the term in the US came to be perceived as covering topics related to unionized firms, unions and collective bargaining only. From the mid-1970s as the rate of unionization declined and de-industrialization began, the field of industrial relations in the US began to be seen as somewhat narrow and outdated. From management's perspective, human resource management covered the entire range of issues that involved the company's relations with, and management of its workforce. Within the US national association, the Industrial Relations Research Association (IRRA), this eventually led to a discussion of a name change on the grounds that the IRRA covered a much broader range of subjects than the name implied. Within the IRRA, this provoked a heated, emotional debate as many long-time members viewed a change of name as a repudiation of the IRRA's commitment to free trade unions, collective bargaining and employee voice. After more than 15 years of debate, the IRRA officially changed its name in 2005 to the Labour and Employment Relations Association (LERA).

At international level, the move to change the name of the International Industrial Relations Association (IIRA) had a different motivation. By the year 2000, those who were attuned to changes in the US, Canada and Australia were aware that the term "industrial relations" in English seemed to have a narrow meaning, much narrower than the coverage of topics at IIRA congresses. Informal discussion began on a new name. The IIRA Secretary, Giuseppe Casale, broached the subject in 2006 and met with an open, non-hostile reception. In the next three years, the issue was debated, most pointedly at the 2007 European regional congress in Manchester. There were those who reacted negatively, in part because the term "industrial relations" did not have such a narrow meaning in many non-English-speaking countries and a change seemed unnecessary. There was also some resistance to a move that might be interpreted as the association abandoning its commitment to the values of a pluralistic system that recognizes the legitimacy of independent employee voice and collective bargaining. In the best traditions of the IIRA, past-presidents were on both sides of the debate. By 2009 there appeared to be a majority in favor of a name change, but no agreement on the name. Some possibilities were ruled out (e.g. already in use by another association, or not susceptible to a good acronym). Finally, International Labour and Employment Relations Association (ILERA) was suggested, not because it was modeled after the American LERA, but because the name conjured up the ILO ("International Labour") and all the topics the ILO covers, because it emphasized "Labour" - people who work and everything connected with work, and "Employment Relations," which indicated that the association would also focus on the employment relationship. The new name, ILERA, was accepted by the executive committee and approved at the 2009 World Congress in Sydney. Forty years after its founding, the association in a sense turned to its other two founding members, the Japan Institute of Labour and the International Institute for Labour Studies (at the ILO) and placed the spotlight on labour as the central point of interest.

The Language of ILERA

In any international association the issue of language crops up. Unlike science or economics associations, ILERA and its sister organization, the International Society for Labour and Social Security Law (ISLSSL), have a particularly challenging situation. Many terms used in industrial relations and labour law have no uniform definition worldwide, even in English. In a sense, terms often describe situations rather than a precise phenomenon. The difficulties in providing simultaneous translation at ILERA congresses were significant as many who listened to plenary session papers through translation can attest.

In its early years, ILERA expected that English, French and Spanish translation would be provided at congresses. Over the years, English became more widely spoken (perhaps because of the internet) to the point where it became evident that most participants at ILERA congresses were able to understand English. In some countries, the ability of congress organizers to assemble competent simultaneous interpreters was very limited, and the cost so high as to make the registration fee for the congress prohibitively expensive for many members. At the executive committee meeting during the 2006 World

Congress in Lima, Peru, the question of language was raised. The 2009 World Congress was scheduled to be held in Sydney, Australia and it was expected that nearly everyone who would attend would be able to speak English. After discussing various options, it was decided that the organizer/host national association of an ILERA world or regional congress would be required to provide English translation, but other than that, it would be the decision of the organizer what other languages would be translated.

In view of the emotion that this issue of language translation has generated at other international associations (such as the ISLSSL) and in governmental organizations (such as the EU), it is to ILERA's immense credit that the member national associations accepted this new language policy as a pragmatic decision which reflected sensitivity to the budgetary concerns of national associations organizing a congress. Since 2006 and the new policy, the issue of language has never arisen. In the world congresses in English-speaking countries (2009 Australia, 2012 United States, 2015 South Africa), translation into no other language has been provided, but attendance has been strong and from many countries. In some non-English-speaking countries where English is widely spoken (at least among academics and professionals), the regional congress has been in English only; for example, 2010 Copenhagen, 2010 Bali, 2011 Lagos. The ILERA policy does give congress organizers discretion on whether to provide translation and some have exercised this discretion. Examples are 2011 São Paulo (Portuguese, Spanish, English), 2014 Bogotá (Spanish-English), and 2016 Beijing (Chinese-English).

The member associations have recognized that the policy set a minimum requirement, but not an expectation that congresses will be in English only. It allows the organizers to assess the need for translation and gives them the ability to respond if resources permit.

The policy could, however, be seen by some as indicating a lack of interest on ILERA's part on certain parts of the world, or a lack of regard for the scholarship of academics in certain countries. This would undermine ILERA's goals of scientific study of labour and employment relations on all continents. It is a potential weakness against which the association's leadership must guard. To guard against linguistic imperialism, ILERA must continue to exercise judicious selection of sites for the world and regional congresses, must take pro-active approaches to ILERA type associations in countries which have not yet joined ILERA, and must constantly scrutinize the themes and session topics at congresses to ensure coverage of issues relevant to the non-English-speaking world.

Expansion of ILERA's Membership

Fifty years ago, ILERA had four members but from three continents. The early congresses reflected the interests of advanced market economies. Some might say "Western" countries (including Japan and Australia), but more accurately the topics at these congresses reflected the interests of developed manufacturing economies. This is not surprising since the field of industrial relations in itself is tied to the industrial revolution and the impact of industrialization on the organization of work, the terms and condition offered workers, and worker opportunities. Over the decades, the membership of ILERA expanded, and with globalization many countries, especially in Asia, embarked on the process of industrialization. As John Niland remarked, the 1992 World Congress marked a major advance for ILERA as it was moving from the northern hemisphere and also to Asia. The venue was symbolic, in itself, of ILERA extending its reach worldwide. Similar in impact was the 2006 World Congress in Lima.

One of the most striking aspects of ILERA's progress has been the ability to bring in new members and adjust programming to meet new interests. Regional congresses have helped enormously in demonstrating to national associations that ILERA has feasible options for participation. Not needing to travel huge distances have made these regional congresses popular to many who would not travel to another continent for a World Congress. The regional focus of the congress has also made the topical programming more targeted and appealing to many.

Perhaps it was the establishment of the World Trade Organization (WTO) in 1995 that heightened ILERA's sense it needed to be more pro-active about membership, but for whatever reason, there was a pivot toward Asia. In 2010, a regional congress was held in Indonesia, which would have been unthinkable only a decade before. In 2012, after a long period of discussion, the People's Republic of China joined, and within four years hosted a regional congress in Beijing, which brought many ILERA members to China for first time.

With the exception of South Africa and Nigeria, ILERA had not found much interest in the continent of Africa. But since 2012, the ILERA Secretary has been active in promoting ways small numbers of persons in different countries interested in ILERA can meet under the ILERA umbrella. Some have been from English-speaking countries in southern Africa, with the South African ILERA affiliate playing a major role in organizing the meetings. More recently, ILERA Secretary Moussa Oumarou has made efforts to stimulate interest in French-speaking Africa.

The challenge at the present time is to balance the interests of those in the most advanced countries who are experiencing de-industrialization with those of newly industrializing countries. In light of the "track" system of topical coverage at world congresses, this balance should be achievable.

The Challenge of Globalization

Much has been written about globalization and the impact of globalization on industrial relations. Often, those discussing this concentrate on the inadequacy of national-level bargaining to control the parameters within which employers and labour work. Forty years ago, some lamented that multinational companies were more powerful than the sovereign state, and attention was directed to supranational responses.[8] The overriding disconnect is that regulation occurs at the national level yet companies do not view their sphere of possibilities as limited by national boundaries. Thus, capital can move across borders easily, but industrial relations systems traditionally have been tied to national systems in part because workers do not move across borders easily and in part because the reach of regulation for the most part is nation based.[9]

There has been less discussion of the sobering implications for unions. A fundamental principle of union organization indicates the magnitude of the challenge. The great American labour economist, John R. Commons of the University of Wisconsin, famously remarked that a union must organize the length and breadth of the market. In other words, a union must be able to take the price of labour out of competition, and it can only do that if it can organize all the workers making the product that will be sold in the same market. Doing research in the US, with its vast internal market and with many states regulating labour, Commons grasped the dilemma. He realized that employers compete with each other, and if a company is selling its product in the same market at a higher price than the same product made by other companies, it will be in trouble. It will seek to lower its price, and one easy way to do this is to slash labour costs. The only way for unions to resist this would be for unions to organize all the workers producing the same product for the same market so that they can be in a position to seek to raise wages. If so, the union can impose higher labour costs on employers. Traditional industrial relations systems in many European and North American countries were developed on the assumption that unions could impose higher labour costs on employers. National labour law regimes regulated and, in fact supported, national industrial relations systems built on that assumption.[10]

A problem immediately arises if companies can sell in the same market, but produce in different labour markets. Here the US was unusual in that its fragmented labour market did mean that companies in the same industry selling in the same market could locate in different labour markets, which had markedly different labour costs.[11] American unions faced this problem from the 1950s and the decline in the rate of unionization begins at that point. For unions in other countries, this problem of companies being able to sell in the same market but producing in some other labour market came later, but it inevitably arose when it was feasible to have the products made in another country, especially if that other country has much lower labour costs. Since the 1980s, technological advances and the dropping of trade barriers have led to the phenomenon dubbed globalization. The most noticeable change has been in the amount of manufactured goods moving from east to west. Although foreign direct investment has increased, the dramatic change has been the sharp increase in the number of domestically owned companies, particularly in Asia and South Asia, which produce goods purchased by companies in Europe and North America. The major industrial-relations problem arises from the fact that in many of these Asian countries, unions barely existed nor did political parties supportive of labour. Many exporting countries had few labour laws, especially any supporting freedom of association and collective bargaining. Even if they did, laws were usually not enforced and in some countries exceptions were made for manufacturing facilities in export processing zones.

Supranational Responses

Although often not acknowledged, one of the reasons behind the ILO's founding in 1919 was the awareness that an improvement in labour standards could not be achieved unless countries in competition with each other agreed upon minimum labour standards.[12] But by the 1990s, although the ILO had been the leading international organization dedicated to just treatment for workers, its primary means of achieving its mission seemed inadequate since it could not order countries to take action and enforce that order. This was a period when human rights activists were demanding fair trade, not simply free trade.[13]

Within the ILO, subsequent to the fall of the Berlin Wall, work began on a declaration that would set out fundamental principles. In retrospect, there were likely different motivations for wanting such a declaration, some of which may have been in conflict. Some believed that a declaration would commit all ILO member states to supporting these fundamental principles and the linked core conventions. Others, especially employers, may have seen the declaration as a way of supporting worker rights in general rather than grappling with precise commitments.[14] For some time, this difference in support for the 1998 ILO Declaration of Fundamental Principles and Rights at Work was papered over. But in a curious way, since the year 2000, soft law may have pushed these differences between workers and employers at the ILO out into the open.

Soft Law on Worker Rights

Within the past 20 years, attention has turned to global supply chains, wherein a company in an advanced economy buys materials or a finished product from an independently owned supplier company in a developing country where wages and labour conditions are often far inferior to that of the purchaser company. Human rights groups have argued that the purchaser company has the ability to require that the supplier company abide by internationally recognized labour standards and these should be included in contracts. This has led to the development of company codes of conduct, and in turn, since 2000 there has been increasing acceptance for the notion that companies, on their own, should comply with international labour standards in all their activities.[15] But what labour standards? Since the 1998 ILO Declaration, the easy answer has been to latch onto the ILO's four enumerated fundamental principles.

First proposed by Kofi Annan in January 1999, the UN Global Compact (UNGC), an initiative of the UN Secretary General's office, was launched on July 26, 2000. The aim was to have companies voluntarily agree to align their strategies and activities with human rights, among which were four relating to labour. These four word-for-word repeat the four fundamental principles of the ILO's 1998 Declaration. Thus, the ILO's tripartite process of producing four fundamental principles was imported into UN soft law. In light of the somewhat vague and imprecise statements in the UNGC, and its non-binding nature, its value might be questioned. But 12,000 companies in 160 countries have signed it.[16] Moreover, most of these companies felt compelled to have a code of conduct (in part perhaps because they were pressured by human rights activists to take a stance), and when they wrote their code and had to make a statement regarding worker rights, they invariably selected the four fundamental principles as proclaimed by the ILO in 1998.[17]

Pushback Against Rights Established in International Law

All of this, however, is soft law. Many supporters of worker rights became disenchanted that more than 15 years of effort had failed to produce something more. The UN became the next forum to consider worker rights. On June 16, 2011, the United Nations Human Rights Council unanimously endorsed the Guiding Principles for the Implementation of the UN "Protect, Respect and Remedy Framework."[18] Using this, Part II of the UN Guiding Principles on Business and Human Rights (UNGP) focuses on the "corporate responsibility to respect human rights" and lists five foundational principles, the first of which declares "Business enterprises should respect human rights."[19] Unlike the UN Global Compact, the UNGP took a position on what it meant by human rights. Included in the list was the 1998 ILO Declaration's four fundamental rights and the eight linked core conventions.

At this point, soft law was beginning to harden, and it may be that employers recognized the threat. When they had agreed in their company codes of conduct to abide by the ILO's four fundamental principles, including freedom of association, did that mean that they accepted that the right to strike was an integral part of freedom of association? This question flared at the 2012 International Labour Conference with the Employers asserting that ILO Convention No. 87, Freedom of Association, does not protect the right to strike.[20] As Manfred Weiss has described in his chapter, a crisis did occur and by 2015 a ceasefire was put into effect,[21] but the issue is not resolved. The issue is extremely significant since many free trade agreements include a labour clause that states that the signatories must abide by certain worker rights,[22] and nowadays, invariably the ILO's four fundamental principles are listed, but not the eight linked core conventions.[23] Moreover, the failure of governments to support fully the understanding of a convention that has been accepted for more than 50 years indicates the power of global capital over governments at this time.

In the industrial relations context, the failure of the ILO tripartite partners to uphold a robust guarantee of freedom of association, one that recognizes the right to strike, is an immense threat. Not only are unions unable to impose higher wage costs if they will be undercut by cheaper labour, but they also will be unable to organize workers. Events in countries such as Bangladesh and Cambodia demonstrate this. Whether unions everywhere will be greatly weakened and wither because of this failure remains a critical issue for the future of industrial relations worldwide.

The Information Age and the Digital Economy

Industrial relations is a result of industrialization. As ILERA looks to the future, the new issues will relate to the immense, disruptive changes that will occur as advanced countries move fully into the Information Age. At the present time, the "gig economy" is the subject of many conferences, but it is only one piece of a larger puzzle.

In the United States, especially in light of the 2016 presidential election, there has been discussion of the more general phenomenon of work becoming more insecure and how this is making it more difficult for people to maintain a middle-class way of life. This sense of unease is found in other countries also, especially in the UK and Europe. This discussion covers many types of work, not only gig economy work. The phenomenon has been identified and critiqued by

David Weil who has decried that the workplace has become "fissured" by which he means that the notion that a person goes to a workplace and works for the company that is located there and is employed directly by that company no longer holds for a large segment of the labour force.[24] Weil systemically sets out the various underlying causes, consequences and policy implications of the multi-layering and piecemeal slicing up of what had been the traditional employer-employee relationship.

Although the available data at present is not useful,[25] several scholars believe that the phenomenon is real. In writing a long review of Weil's book, Richard Freeman agreed with Weil's conclusions, but noted that the result (a wide variation in compensation for workers with the same skills between firms in the same industry) is not what standard economic theory regarding wage determination would predict. Freeman comments that "either our models misrepresent the way a relatively unfettered labour market works in reality or we are missing important market forces in applying the model."[26] This pinpoints an area where important research is needed.

Average people know that their lifestyle depends on having a job, and preferably one with decent wages and working conditions and a modicum of security. Their anxiety, often based on anecdotal evidence, relates to the availability of such jobs. This anxiety is not unfounded. Central bankers have been perplexed by the failure of wages to rise even when unemployment levels are low. One highly respected institution has cited slack in the labour market as the explanation.[27] Commenting that country-level data appears to be understating involuntary part time working, the International Monetary Fund (IMF) also pointed to slow productivity growth.[28] The fact that the skill level of workers is not being fully utilized may explain the slow growth. This phenomenon does not jump out from the statistics because workers may be working full-time, but at a job that does not call upon their skills.[29] In many countries, the supply of educated persons may be higher than current demand in higher wage service industries.

At the same time new information technologies have been eliminating middle-skill jobs. Studies on the long-term effects of new technologies automating mental work do not find across-the-board negative effects, but they do find larger effects on the wages of particular groups, such as middle-skilled workers.[30] The IMF suggests that even low-skilled workers may have been negatively affected in that they see to have experienced a larger decline in hours than other skill groups.[31]

Topics such as unemployment (cyclical or structural), full employment, job training, and social safety nets have appeared regularly on ILERA programs. They will remain timely in the new digital economy, but they may be different. It may be that our concept of full-time employment is obsolete as we move into an era when so much more can be produced in so much less time by so many fewer people. But it will be daunting political task to de-couple the link between work and income and to re-set the formula for how income is distributed. This is a policy question, and one that implicates values as Tom Kochan's contribution points out. ILERA has always engaged in policy issues and the digital economy will require new thinking and innovative recommendations if working people are to maintain stable lives.

Although less studied by ILERA members, how companies organize work and employ people has been a regular topic. The game changer in the last few years has been the rapid introduction of "algorithms" in business. This technological development has made possible the modern gig economy whereby someone desiring a service can be connected with a person willing to perform the service with both user and performer connecting through a platform driven by artificial intelligence (AI). This has led to a paradigm shift in the orientation of capital. Companies using the platform to match customer demand for a service with a worker willing to perform that service have reconceptualized the internal organization of the company. This type of company no longer needs a human resources department that advertises jobs, screens applicants and selects from among them. Instead a description of the services wanted, and an application form is placed online. An algorithm selects who will be offered a position. It no longer needs supervisors. Once selected, the worker has no supervisor and is not subjected to performance reviews. It needs no marketing staff considering pricing, or operations managers matching demand for the service with supply. An algorithm monitors the demand for the service and the providers willing to meet that demand at any given moment, and it sets the price the end user will pay. The providers/workers know of work opportunities through an app. They are instructed on what to do (where to go) by the app. Their performance is rated by the end users through an app. The provider may be de-selected by the platform based on these ratings which are analyzed by an algorithm. Researchers have focused on those who work (provide the services) for these new platform-based, gig economy companies. What is truly paradigm shifting is the lack of middle level staff. There are workers, and there are very high level managers and programmers but the middle is empty. That too may be a challenge for society, the lack of jobs for the middle class, but at present labour force statistics are not capturing those who are not there. Once again, research is needed on this new situation, including a consideration of how the definition of labour force categories and the collection of data are accurately capturing what is happening in the labour market.

Policy questions abound. In this new gig economy, traditional notions of industrial employment are often irrelevant. This type of work, managed by an algorithm, usually does not require set working hours. Compensation is related to the unit of work performed (an Uber ride, a Grubhub food delivery, a task on Amazon Mechanical Turk). It is the work done on a piece rate basis, often with workers competing to secure the work opportunity on a crowdsourcing basis.

This is not new - piece work was a hallmark of early industrialization. In itself it may be acceptable, but from an overall societal viewpoint, the problem arises when attempting to determine whether working hours are excessive or unpredictable. How can work-life balance be planned, let alone maintained? How can workers predict their earnings and their schedule so as to plan child care arrangements and make housing commitments (month rent or mortgage payments)? At present, many of these questions are viewed as labour law questions, if only because existing labour laws seemingly do not apply, for instance to Uber drivers, or because employers are seen as skirting the law (by incorrectly categorizing these workers as independent contractors). But it may be more useful to recognize that labour laws written for the industrial age simply do not fit information age work. Labour lawyers (including several former ILERA presidents) have often benefited from their exposure through ILERA to labour economics and industrial relations research which has given them insights on how to craft better labour law responses. The digital economy promises to present many such questions. Most importantly, ILERA's labour law scholars must not cling to industrial age notions of rights, but must focus on fundamental values such as the dignity and autonomy of individuals and must devise new laws that protect these values in this new tech-enabled world.

Conclusion

While at times the issues of the current day and the near future appear threatening, for ILERA with its tradition of multidisciplinary engagement and its commitment to research and the sharing of knowledge, the future is bright. We are moving into a new age, a digital economy. The problems this disruptive change will create are problems that will affect most people in society, and are of huge importance. If ILERA holds true to its traditions and mission, if it continues to reach out worldwide, younger scholars and practitioners will see its value and inject new vitality into its work.

Notes

1 Paper prepared for the past-presidents' session commemorating the 50th Anniversary of the International Labour and Employment Relations Association (ILERA), 18th World Congress of the ILERA, Seoul, Korea, July 23-27, 2018.

2 Maupain, Francis (2013) *The Future of the International Labour Organization in the Global Economy*, Hart Publishing, p. 2.

3 In 1967, this group changed its name to the British Universities Industrial Relations Association (BUIRA). Berridge, J. and Goodman, J.F.B. (1988) "The British Universities Industrial Relations Association: The First 35 Years," *British Journal of Industrial Relations*, 26, pp. 155-177.

4 Kaufman, Bruce E. (2004) *The Global Evolution of Industrial Relations*, International Labour Office, p. 85.

5 One of the most notorious incidents occurred in 1914 in southern Colorado as part of a more than year-long effort to unionize the coal miners at several companies, the largest of which were

controlled by the Rockefeller family. Striking miners and their families had been evicted from company housing and were living in tent compounds. In December 1914, the state militia advanced on striking workers from the Colorado Iron and Fuel Company who fought back. More than a dozen persons were killed, including many women and children. In the days following, the strikers retaliated and attacked non-union sites and more people were killed.

6 Dunlop, John (1958) *Industrial Relations Systems*, Holt.

7 Kaufman, op. cit. discusses this point and observes that the "disjunction between Anglo-American and European perspectives goes far deeper than just language" resulting from "differences in *institutions, ideologies* and the *conceptualization* given to the subject matter of industrial relations" (p. 437).

8 Examples would be the OECD Guidelines for Multinational Enterprises, adopted in 1976 and most recently revised in May 2011, and the ILO'S Tripartite Principles Concerning Transnational Enterprises and Social Policy. The latter was adopted by the Governing Body of the International Labour Office at its 204th Session in November 1977, and was amended at its 279th Session in November 2000. http://www.ilo.org/wcmsp5/groups/public/@ed_emp/@emp_ent/documents/publication/wcms_101234.pdf.

9 The European Union is the one region where the member states have relinquished significant regulatory capacity to the center.

10 There are different ways of doing this. The most striking example is found in Europe where some countries allow the extension of collective agreements to non-signatory employers in an industry.

11 As early as the 1950s, unions in the US were contending with labour intensive industries moving to the Southern part of the

country in search of lower labour costs and less union friendly environments.

12 The British civil servant who in 1918 wrote the proposal that would, within months, become Part XIII of the Treaty of Versailles establishing the ILO, expressly recognized this. Edward Phelan's first degree was in economics, and he had spent his first years as a civil servant researching cost of living and wage rates in Scotland. See Chapter 6, "The birth of the International Labour Organization," in International Labour Office (2009). *Edward Phelan and the ILO: The Life and Views of an International Social Actor* (pp. 137-183). Geneva: ILO.

13 The effort to have the WTO link trading privileges to observance of worker rights failed. The WTO said worker rights was the province of the ILO. S*ingapore WTO Ministerial 1996: Ministerial Declaration, WT/MIN (96)/Dec*, December 18, 1996. Available at http://www. wto. org/english/thewto_e/minist_e/min96_e/wtodec_e. htm

14 For a discussion, see Bellace, Janice R. (2016) "Back to the Future: Freedom of Association, the Right to Strike and National Law," *King's Law Journal*, 27(1), pp. 1-22, at pp. 13-15.

15 The UN Global Compact was first announced by UN Secretary General Kofi Annan in a speech to the World Economic Forum in January 1999. It was launched in July 2000. http://www. unglobalcompact. org/.

16 https://www. unglobalcompact. org/participation.

17 The lack of specific definitions of critical terms aroused skepticism among critics of corporate codes of conduct. See, e. g. Diller, Janelle (1999) "A Social Conscience in the Global Marketplace? Labour Dimensions of Codes of Conduct, Social Labeling and Investor Initiatives," *International Labour Review*, 138(2), pp. 99-129. See also Alston, Philip (2005) "Facing Up to the Complexities of the ILO's Core Labour Standards Agenda," *The European Journal of*

International Law, 16, p. 467.

18 United Nations, Human Rights Council, Seventeenth session, Agenda item 3: Report of the Special Representative of the Secretary-General on the issue of human rights and transnational corporations and other business enterprises, John Ruggie. Adoption of Resolution, 17/4, Human rights and transnational corporations and other business enterprises. June 16, 2011, A/HRC/17/31. The Guiding Principles are found in the Annex to this report, p. 6-27. Accessible at http://www.ohchr.org/Documents/Issues/Business/A-HRC-17-31_AEV.pdf.

19 Ibid., p. 13.

20 For an exposition of this view, see International Organization of Employers, *Do ILO Conventions 87 and 98 Recognise a Right to Strike?* (October 2014) at 10. www.ilo.org/public/english/bureau/leg/download/ioe_conventions_87_and_98.pdf.

21 Final report of the Meeting. Tripartite Meeting on the Freedom of Association and Protection of the Right to Organise Convention, 1948 (No. 87), in relation to the right to strike and the modalities and practices of strike action at national level. February 23-25, 2015. ILO, Geneva. http://www.ilo.org/wcmsp5/groups/public/@ed_norm/@relconf/documents/meetingdocument/wcms_349069.pdf.

22 The EU and US free trade agreements differ on whether the fundamental rights link to ILO conventions. For a discussion, see Agusti-Panareda, Jordi, Ebert, Franz Christian and LeClerq, Desirée (2015) “ILO Labour Standards and Trade Agreements: A Case for Consistency,” *Comparative Labour Law and Policy Journal*, 36(2) (Spring), pp. 347-380.

23 The Trans-Pacific Partnership is a leading example of this. Chapter 19, section 19.3, footnote 3. Once the US withdrew from the TPP, the other 11 continued and in March 2018 signed the Comprehensive Progressive Trans-Pacific Partnership. The 11 countries are Australia, Brunei, Canada, Chile, Japan, Malaysia, Mexico, New Zealand, Peru,

Singapore and Vietnam. The labour chapter remained the same.

24 Weil, David (2014) *The Fissured Workplace: Why Work Became So Bad for So Many and What Can Be Done to Improve It*, Harvard University Press.

25 This results from the fact that the conceptualization of how labour force information should be captured relates to a past era. For instance, from government published labour statistics, usually it is impossible to tell if a full-time janitorial worker is employed by the company that is the main company in the building or by some other company.

26 Freeman, Richard B. (2014) "The Subcontracted Labour Market: David Weil's Book, The Fissured Workplace, Describes a Disturbing Trend for Workers," *Perspectives on Work*, 18, pp 38-41 (http://www.fissuredworkplace.net/assets/LabourMarket_mf.pdf).

27 International Monetary Fund (2017) "Seeking Sustainable Growth: Short-Term Recovery, Long-Term Challenges." Chapter 2, *World Economic Outlook*, (October) pp. 73-116.

28 Ibid. The report notes that at the country level, labour market slack, together with weak productivity growth and low inflation expectations, are the main forces weighing on wage growth (p. 90).

29 Valletta, Robert G. (2016) *Recent Flattening in the Higher Education Wage Premium: Polarization, Skill Downgrading, or Both?* NBER Working Paper 22935, National Bureau of Economic Research.

30 Autor, David H. and Dorn, David (2013) "The Growth of Low-Skill Services Jobs and the Polarization of the US Labour Market," *American Economic Review*, 103(5), pp. 1553-1597.

31 International Monetary Fund, op. cit, p. 92. The IMF notes that country-level data by sector on hours by skill level are not readily available. It may be that there has been a decline in one sector, such as retail, but not in another, such as nursing

homes/personal care.

References

Agusti-Panareda, Jordi, Ebert, Franz Christian and LeClerq, Desirée (2015) "ILO Labour Standards and Trade Agreements: A Case for Consistency," *Comparative Labour Law and Policy Journal* (Spring), 36(2), pp. 347-380.

Alston, Philip (2005) "Facing Up to the Complexities of the ILO's Core Labour Standards Agenda," *The European Journal of International Law*, 16, p. 467.

Autor, David H. and Dorn, David (2013), "The Growth of Low-Skill Services Jobs and the Polarization of the US Labour Market," *American Economic Review*, 103(5), pp. 1553-1597.

Bellace, Janice R. (2016) "Back to the Future: Freedom of Association, the Right to Strike and National Law," *King's Law Journal*, 27(1), pp. 1-22.

Berridge, J. and Goodman, J.F.B. (1988) "The British Universities Industrial Relations Association: The First 35 Years," *British Journal of Industrial Relations*, 26, pp. 155-177.

Diller, Janelle (1999) "A Social Conscience in the Global Marketplace? Labour Dimensions of Codes of Conduct, Social Labeling and Investor Initiatives," *International Labour Review*, 138(2), pp. 99-129.

Dunlop, John. (1958), *Industrial Relations Systems*, Holt.

Freeman, Richard B. (2014) "The Subcontracted Labour Market: David Weil's Book, The Fissured Workplace, Describes a Disturbing Trend for Workers," *Perspectives on Work*, 18, pp. 38-41 (http://www.fissuredworkplace.net/assets/LabourMarket_mf.pdf).

International Labour Office (2009) "The Birth of the International Labour Organization," in Edward Phelan and the ILO: *The Life and Views of an International Social Actor*, ILO, pp. 137-183.

International Monetary Fund (2017), "Seeking Sustainable Growth: Short-Term Recovery, Long-Term Challenges," *World Economic Outlook* (October), pp. 73-116.

International Organization of Employers, (2014) *Do ILO Conventions 87 and 98 Recognise a Right to Strike?* (October) (www.ilo.org/public/english/bureau/leg/download/ioe_conventions_87_and_98.pdf).

Kaufman, Bruce E. (2004) *The Global Evolution of Industrial Relations*, International Labour Office.

Maupain, Franics (2013) *The Future of the International Labour Organization in the Global Economy*, Hart.

Valletta, Robert G. (2016) *Recent Flattening in the Higher Education Wage Premium: Polarization, Skill Downgrading, or Both?* NBER Working Paper 22935, National Bureau of Economic Research, Cambridge, MA.

Weil, David (2014) *The Fissured Workplace: Why Work Became So Bad for So Many and What Can Be Done to Improve It*, Harvard University Press.

ILERA and the Future of Work: Challenges and Opportunities in the Quest for Universal Decent Work and Social Solidarity

Evance Kalula

10

> Had I been present at the creation I would have given some useful hints for the better ordering of the Universe
>
> (Alphonso X, the Learned, King of Spain, 1252-1284)

Introduction

The opportunity to serve as President of ILERA has undoubtedly been the highest honor of my academic and professional career; following in the footsteps of giants in our field has been an incredible privilege. The privilege of having served as ILERA president is the more profound on account of not only joining the ranks of scholars that I admire, but having among them, in Manfred Weiss, a personal mentor and a committed friend of Africa who has encouraged and mentored scores of young professionals and scholars for almost a generation now. Not least in their remarkable service have been the ILERA Secretariat. Three of them, among them two fellow African compatriots, Tayo Fashoyin and Moussa Oumarou, who have served as secretary to our association, along with Johanna de Vries as administrator, they have made invaluable contributions to ILERA. My colleagues in Africa, particularly those whose tireless efforts made good the opportunity Africa was given to host the 17th World Congress for the first time, led by Frikkie de Bruin made it possible to make a good success of it. I sincerely pay tribute to them all for their inspiration and service to our association.

It is befitting that both the ILERA 18th Congress and the 50th anniversary are being held in Korea, it is a significant twin celebration of what is possible for countries to make progress in the face of intense adversity. It is particularly remarkable when it is considered that economic and social indicators for Korea were not exceptionally different from many other developing countries in the 1960s. The Korean experience is therefore an enduring and positive example to other countries grappling with the challenges of underdevelopment.

As ILERA President, I sought to confirm and reinforce the universality of what our association stands for, that in the world of work and the pursuit of our field there are common endeavors that are worth pursuing to engender common purpose and progress. Our association, made up as it is of different disciplines and actors in the guise of not only scholars but a diverse range of practitioners and professionals, including human resource, industrial relations, policy makers and trade unionists drawn from all regions of the world emphasizes inclusivity in diversity. It is to some of those endeavors in terms of challenges and opportunities that I would like to briefly focus on in this contribution.

Please allow me to use Africa as a proxy, but I must hasten to add that many of the issues I seek to canvass are not unique to Africa. However, they present to me with an intensity and immediacy of a lived experience and continuous reflection.

Some Reflections

And so to my brief reflection on the future of work, challenges and opportunities. Globalization and its attendant consequences have changed the world of work immensely, some might say forever.

The 17th ILERA World Congress in 2015 over which I was privileged to preside as president had "The Changing World of Work: Implications for Labour and Employment Relations, and Social Protection" as its theme. To my mind what was addressed amply reflects both the legacy and the future endeavors of ILERA. The Congress dwelt on a broad range of critical issues concerning the current and future challenges, and opportunities in the world of work, and therefore the domain of our association.

A sample of the sessions of the Congress amply show the rich diversity of engagement. Issues covered encompassed the entire scope of our field ranging from, to cite some instances, traditional matters of employment relations, human resources, law and labour market regulation, equality and equity, labour migration, conflict and disputes at work, innovation, social protection and unemployment.

From these I would like to draw out a few that I think help to define where the world of work has been, currently is and headed for in the ever-changing world of work, using as I indicated above, Africa as a proxy of global concerns.

A number of areas that prominently featured at the 17th Congress and continue to be prevalent issues in the changing world of work stand out. They flow from historical and contemporary developments, including the impact of globalization, inequities of current economic arrangements which relate to inequality, migration, exclusion and poverty, and lack of adequate social solidarity. In highlighting elements in the world of work, there can be no better source of articulation of the issues than various International Labour Organization (ILO) programs in which the future of work is central, in particular the Decent Work Programme. The ILO's central concern with the future of work is clearly apparent from its establishment in 2017 of the 28-member Global Commission on the Future of Work. The Commission has been charged with the task of "assessing the rapid transformations taking place in the world of work, and identifying the key challenges and what must make the future of work better and fairer" (ILO, 2017). Whether the Commission's recommendations, when they come forth, will be taken notice of is not certain, but what is certain is that these are concerns central to our mandate as ILERA, to engage with from various vantage points of our field.

Labour Market Regulation

A prime element of one of the causes of the failure to grapple with the changing world of work is the nature of labour markets and inability of regulation to sufficiently take account of changes.

While critical factors, such as innovation and how output is generated are important, there are several issues that stand out which I shall focus on. They relate to migration, the challenge of labour market regulation in a changed environment, unemployment (particularly youth and women's unemployment), increasing inequality, exclusion and poverty, and the search for viable social protection. I would like to focus on some of these briefly and in an eclectic manner as illustrations of challenges and opportunities underpinning the future of work. These are also areas which provide for ILERA contribution and a platform for an enduring legacy.

Africa is a prime example of the effects of the changed and still changing world of work. As I have indicated elsewhere (Kalula, 2003), I came of age in the heady 1970s when a lot seemed possible for Africa and other developing polities. Like in many other respects however, challenges in the world of work quickly emerged as impediments. The received framework of labour market regulation and institutions were particular constraints. The legislation and other instruments of regulation that were inherited at independence were not geared toward the circumstances in developing countries which were markedly different from the former colonial metropolitan countries. The cut and paste reforms carried out, symptomatic of "borrowing and bending" approaches (Thompson, 1993), were and have not been adequate. Such constraints have been worsened with the drastic decline in formal employment and the burgeoning informal economy. Everywhere in Africa and in many developing countries, labour market regulatory instruments and institutions are not only inappropriate in the main but not effectively implemented on account of various factors, not least inadequate institutional capacity and political will.

Social Protection

The situation is similar in respect of social protection. The social solidarity based on the ILO traditional platform that targets the nine risks has proven inadequate. To the ILO's credit however, that shortfall in social protection has been recognized and some steps are being taken to address the situation. Such relatively recent measures as the *Social Protection Floors Recommendation, 2012* are such an attempt. The ILO now estimates that only 0.23% of the world's GDP would be required to give effect to basic floor social protection of about 700 million people of the world's population. That would translate into 10% of the world's vulnerable population getting critical basic floor social protection from only 0.23% of the global GDP. Put differently, no country is too poor to afford to provide basic needs to its population. And yet access to basic needs such as health remains a challenge, for instance about 140 million people in the Caribbean and Latin America, not to mention Africa, lack such access. However, much work needs to be done to generate evidence-based research to affirm alternative modes of social protection and extend coverage to the informal sector. There can be no doubt that this is an area that ILERA, through individual and collective efforts, ought to be preoccupied with.

Unemployment

Unemployment, particularly among the youth and women is a definite scourge that now is a given and central to the future of the world of work. Unemployment is one of the main drivers of inequality, poverty, gender discrimination, not to mention migration and inadequate protection of vulnerable workers, among other consequences. It is also due to the inability of traditional forms of regulation and social protection. In many countries, in Africa for instance, formal employment is less than 10%. About 66% of working women in Sub-Saharan Africa are in the agricultural sector, mostly in the labour-intensive informal economy. Even the few women that are employed in the formal sector, inequality in conditions of work and remuneration is the norm. The situation of the youth is just as bad, 66 million of the world's unemployed are young people, and about 145 million youth in employment live in poverty. Similarly, social solidarity in the form of social security is mainly through social insurance covering a tiny minority in the formal sector. And yet 66% of working people in Africa (52% in North Africa) are employed in the informal sector and lack social protection because of their status. The need is not simply to find alternative and innovative approaches to create forms of occupation geared toward the post-industrial realities, but promote decent work wherever work in any form is undertaken and with it critical social protection, particularly in non-formal situations.

Migration

Migration is almost as old as the human race itself. It is a given that, but for migration, different civilizations that have come and gone in human history would not have come about. Migration has been the fabric with which human history has been woven. No single source of human activity has defined both opportunity and tragedy so dramatically. The impact of migration has been and continues to be enormous, it has been a major factor driving globalization. In 2012, it was estimated that up to 3% of the world population, about 230 million people live outside their countries of origin. An even bigger number, of about 763 million people live outside their countries of birth. Migration comes in multiple guises, the most notorious instances are of course the current South to North migration, highlighted by Africa to Europe across the Mediterranean, and the earlier boat people from Asia to Australasia. However, there are equally other tragic migration forms, internal country and intra-continental. In Africa and many other developing countries including China, for example, the phenomenon of migration has tremendous relevance to labour markets, not to mention broader human rights considerations, it is apparent in the rural to urban drift and conflict situations. As always, children and women bear most of the suffering, as child soldiers and labour, and women abused along with them. The drama continues to unfold before us and is intrinsically linked to ILERA's focal areas of engagement, that is to say globalization, human solidarity, exclusion, opportunity, poverty and the future of work itself. Not to put too fine a point on it, the consequences of migration are dramatic and deserve a central place in the deliberations of our association.

Conclusion

On becoming 50, our association reached an important milestone; it has truly come of age. ILERA has facilitated invaluable contributions from our members in our field worldwide. The diversity of our disciplines and membership consisting as it does of academics, practitioners and professionals in human resources, industrial and labour law has served us well. However, there is a lot to be done with lots of challenges to be overcome and opportunities to heighten our contribution. What then would I see as the future that could build on what we have done and enhance our role?

Developing the Next Generation

A number of areas instantly come to mind. The first that comes to mind is the need not only to pass on the legacy of our ideals but to "grow the future timber," that is to say encourage the development of young practitioners, professionals and scholars. The study groups are key, it is imperative to revive them. I cut my teeth as a young scholar from my first participation at the IIRA Paris Congress sitting at the feet of the masters (they were virtually all men) in study groups. It is therefore gratifying that our President Dong-One, has plans to rejuvenate the study groups, they are key to the development of future leaders in our field. Equally important are forms of recognition, such as prizes and other incentives which encourage and recognize emerging talent.

Networks and Collaboration

Beyond ILERA itself, there are lots of initiatives and networks throughout the regions in similar endeavors which focus on the world of work, investigating various aspects of the labour markets, social solidarity and the future of work. An example from Africa is the Southern African Social Protection Experts Network (SASPEN) led by Marius Olivier and others with whom I have been privileged to be associated. Such networks as SASPEN not only make invaluable contribution to new knowledge production in our field, but also contribute to persuading policy makers, particularly in developing countries where institutions are still fragile with inadequate capacity, to the importance of evidence-based policy making and implementation. Similarly farther afield, the Labour Law Research Network (LLRN) has emerged as an effective benchmarking and comparative platform for research relevant to our field.

ILO Partnership

This contribution would not be complete without mentioning the role of the ILO has played in our journey over the last 50 years. The ILO was in a manner of speaking "present at the creation," since then they have not only been our most generous benefactors but they shared our objectives and in effect have been our partners.

The ILO is well placed to help us retool our endeavors for the future of work and social protection. As an organization, the ILO has been at the forefront of responding to the changing world of work. Their reflections that have led to new thinking apparent in their Decent Work Programme and critique of globalization in their seminal report on the Social Dimension of Globalization are prime instances of responses that aim to reposition the organization for the future of work.

The conclusion of the Memorandum of Understanding (MoU) between ILERA and the ILO not only formalizes our relationship, it offers us scope to heighten our collaboration. I dare say that with the well-deserved elevation of "one of us," in Moussa Oumarou, our former Secretary, prospects for closer cooperation are promising.

Enhancing Universality

From its inception as IIRA, our association had implicit global ambitions and has made a lot of progress in that respect. We are now active in every region and striving to grow. A couple of recent developments, with the formal extension of membership to the People's Republic of China and the opening up of the "new Europe," we are now truly a global and diverse international association.

This is indeed good progress, but we still have much to do in promoting diversity and extending membership within regions. Africa is a typical example, prospects of growing ILERA are very good. However, there are quite a number challenges to overcome, not least in the diversification of membership beyond anglophone Africa, to embrace francophone, lusophone and North Africa. Moussa, as ILERA Secretary, had a vision I fully shared as president, to extend membership to other regions of Africa, particularly francophone countries in West Africa where a network is already in place. The establishment of the African Continental Assembly with the aim to drive ILERA activities is a welcome work in progress.

The Future Beckons

And so, as we look forward to the next 50 years and beyond, it could be said that a good start has been made by our association, which has laid a sound foundation for our association to continue and enhance our contribution to the future of the world of work and social solidarity.

In the pursuit of our common endeavors, the Decent Work agenda and quest for universal solidarity through a needs-based social protection deserve a central place. It is an agenda that is both feasible and necessary. Our association was only established in 1966 as IIRA, we could therefore have not been "present at the creation," but as an association we could still "give some useful hints for the better ordering" of the future of work and social protection.

Acknowledgment

The following sources, among others, are gratefully acknowledged.

Bibliography

Fenwick, Colin, Kalula, Evance (2004) "Law and Labour Market Regulation in East Asia and Southern Africa: Comparative Perspectives," *Development and Labour Monographs* 2/2004, Cape Town.

ILERA (2015) The Changing World of Work: Implications for Labour and Employment Relations and Social Protection, *17th World Congress*, Cape Town.

ILO (nd) *Global Commission on the Future of Work* (http://www.ilo.org/global/aboutthe-ilo/newsroom/news/WCM_628749/lang--en/index.htm).

ILO (2008) *Declaration on Social Justice for a Fair Globalization*, Geneva.

ILO (2004) *World Commission on the Social Dimension of Globalization, A Fair Globalization: Creating Opportunities For All.*

ILO (2012) International Labour Conference, "The Youth Employment Crisis: Time for Action," Committee on Youth Employment, 101st Session.

ILO (2015) Transition from Informal to Formal Economy.

ILO (2016) World Employment and Social Outlook Report.

ILO (2017) *The Future of Work We Want: A Global Dialogue*. Geneva, April 6-7 (https://www.ilo.org/wcmsp5/groups/public/---dgreports/---cabinet/

documents/publication/wcms_570282. pdf).

ILO (2017) *Employment and Decent Work for Peace and Resilience Recommendation*, No 205.

Kalula, Evance (2003) "Present at the Creation or Another False Start in Africa? Labour Market Regulation, Social Protection and the Future of Labour Law in Southern Africa," *Professorial Inaugural Lecture*, University of Cape Town.

Kalula, Evance (2014) "Beyond Borrowing and Bending: Labour Market Regulation and the Future of Labour Law in Southern Africa," *Liber Amicorum for Bob Hepple.*

Marius Olivier (2014) "Social Security in the SADC Region and Future Prospects for Coordination, in Social Security and Migrant Workers," *Kluwer International BV*, Netherlands.

Thompson, Clive (1993) "Borrowing and Bending: The Developing of South Africa's Unfair Labour Practice Jurisprudence," in Roger Blanpain and Manfred Weiss (eds.), *The Changing Face of Labour Law and Industrial Relations: Liber Amicorum for Clyde Summers*, Nomos.

Conclusion: Exploring Strategies for Labour and Employment Relations as an Academic Field

Dong-One Kim

11

Introduction

The academic field of labour and employment relations (LER) is currently in turmoil. Because of decreasing union density and collective bargaining coverage in most developed countries (Visser, 2006), there are growing doubts that LER is relevant to the changing employment environment (Budd, 2004; Jensen, 2011; Kaufman, 2008; Kim and Kim, 2018). This concluding chapter examines how LER researchers have responded to and discussed strategic options and the future implications for the field.

There exist two competing views on the evolution of LER. On the one hand, pessimists holding the "change or perish" view argue that the field has not sufficiently evolved in alignment with the increasingly dynamic world of work. Although the world of work has become more complex, they assert that LER remains excessively focused on unions and collective bargaining. Some even go so far as to argue that LER will become irrelevant and disappear if LER remains exclusively focused on its current research agenda. The implication of this "change or perish" view is the clear need for a radical shift in and expansion of the direction of LER research. For example, Kaufman (2008) argued that for LER to survive and prosper in the future, the field needs to greatly broaden its scope.

Conversely, optimists arguing for "maintaining the status quo" assert that LER is slowly, yet steadily, adapting to the changing world of work. For example, researchers are focusing on new forms of collective bargaining, non-union employee representation, gender issues, and LER under globalization. Moreover, despite the stagnation of trade unions and collective bargaining in most developed countries, they continue to assert that unions and collective bargaining still remain central to labour relations. Some even express confidence that unions will rebound and accordingly assert that the essence of LER research must be preserved (Hyman, 2007; Kelly, 1998). Therefore, optimists conclude that no radical redirection from the present is warranted. Thus, currently there is much contention as to the future direction of the study of LER.

In the following, I will explain the trend analyses of LER research in the last decades, discuss various strategic options for LER as an academic field, and seek a viable strategic option for LER.

What We have Done: Trend Analyses of LER Research, 1947-2014

To resolve this debate and shed light on the future direction of LER research, one should first examine what we did in the past to obtain some implications for what we should pursue in the future. A study by Kim and Kim (2018) analyzed the abstracts in major LER journals in the post-World War II era (1947-2014). The data of this analyses include all abstracts available in five representative journals in the field of LER representing four Western countries: Australia, Canada, the UK, and the US. The five journals are the *British Journal of Industrial Relations* (BJIR) from the UK, *Industrial & Labour Relations Review* (ILRR) and *Industrial Relations: A Journal of Economy and Society* (IR) from the US, *Journal of Industrial Relations* (JIR) from Australia, and *Relations Industrielles / Industrial Relations* (RI/IR) from Canada.

First, the frequency of keyword appearance was analyzed. Surprisingly, the number of studies researching trade unions has grown more or less steadily since the 1940s. Specifically, the number of studies dealing with general topics about unions remained stable, but topics about union decline or union revitalization have been on the rise since the 1980s. Therefore, the total number of studies on trade unionism continued to rise. Likewise, other traditional topics in LER, such as collective bargaining, strikes, mediation and arbitration show little sign of declining.[1] Although some of the coefficients were negative, they were statistically insignificant. Although research in LER seemed to increasingly embrace new phenomena and new realities, the number of studies on new topics, such as non-union, temporary and contingent workers, family, gender, women and immigrants rose only marginally. We also found that research in LER was increasingly associated with human resources management (HRM), while maintaining its traditional relationship with economics and law.

Second, utilizing co-occurrence matrix analysis commonly used to quantitatively examine network relationships among data, the relationships among the 20 most frequent keywords over 8 decades (1940s-2010s) were investigated. Table 11.1 shows that the field evolved, but maintained its core: although some conventional topics (e.g. strike, industrial) declined in their rankings or disappeared entirely from the top 20 keywords, most traditional topics (e.g. union, wage, relations) consistently remained top rankers, Although new LER topics (e.g. women, job, workplace) received growing attention from academia, they were not included as top rankers. The field orientation was revealed to have shifted from economics to management, from state to market, and from collective labour to individual employees.

Table 11.1 Top 20 keywords by decade

Rank	Keywords							
	1940s	1950s	1960s	1970s	1980s	1990s	2000s	2010s
1	**labour**	**union**	**Labour**	**union**	**union**	**union**	**union**	**union**
2	**union**	**labour**	**Union**	industri	industri	industri	employ	work
3	relat	industri	industri	**labour**	relat	relat	worker	employ
4	industri	relat	Wage	relat	wage	wage	work	worker
5	**bargain**	wage	Relat	wage	**labour**	worker	wage	**labour**
6	manag	worker	State	**bargain**	employ	employ	relat	relat
7	organ	employ	employ	employ	worker	**labour**	**labour**	employe
8	wage	**bargain**	develop	state	work	firm	industri	wage
9	employ	state	worker	unit	**bargain**	work	employe	industri
10	problem	organ	econom	worker	job	job	job	job
11	econom	econom	Unit	unemploy	**strike**	employe	workplac	firm
12	act	collect	**bargain**	collect	model	**bargain**	market	new
13	**strike**	problem	problem	system	system	manag	new	**bargain**
14	worker	trade	public	public	market	Market	manag	workplac
15	**arbitr**	movement	collect	employe	**arbitr**	New	system	collect
16	collect	act	organ	model	manag	Product	firm	organ
17	product	program	present	develop	develop	Women	practic	research
18	state	issu	unemploy	polici	polici	System	associ	practic
19	plan	develop	market	econom	new	Signific	organ	market
20	disput	present	polici	determine	**women**	Polici	develop	**women**

Overall, the empirical results show that LER research is still largely dominated by union-related topics. These results suggest that most scholars in this field tacitly follow the optimistic view of maintaining the status quo. The overriding question is whether the current level of emphasis on unions and collective bargaining is desirable. I argue otherwise.

Dimensions of Academic Disciplines and LER

In general, academic disciplines can be broadly assessed in three dimensions: significance of subject; existence of a paradigm (Kuhn, 1996); and practical relevance (Biglan, 1973, Cox et al., 2012).
First, for any discipline to survive, the subject should be of significance to society. The best example is the academic field of mining in developed countries. As the number of mines in advanced countries decreased, the academic discipline of mining declined as well (McDivitt, 2002). If the significance of the content declines in real social terms, the field is likely to run the risk of sliding into irrelevance and becoming merely an academic plaything within a narrow academic circle in the short run, and probably become moribund in the long run.

In the case of LER, labour issues, rather than declining, remain or are becoming increasingly important to nearly every society. Heightened competition in product and service markets arising from globalization and rapidly changing technology have led to creative destruction of traditional industries accompanied by restructuring and layoffs. Consequently, we see labour-related headlines in mass media and even SNS (social networking service) on a daily basis. There is no doubt that the subject of this field, labour problems, remains central to the contemporary society (Delaney, 2006).

Second, according to Kuhn (1996), a paradigm is a set of unique beliefs shared by an academic community that regulates scientific research by generating and solving research questions. Without a paradigm, the academic field will not be recognized by other academic fields as either rigorous or providing unique contributions to intellectual progress. Good examples include alchemy and astrology, whose paradigms were rejected and discarded because of their pre-scientific origins and the absence of robustness. On the other hand, LER is centered around the paradigm of cooperation and conflict in employment relations intersecting the domains of politics, economics and society (Kochan, 1998). Within LER exist three prevailing, robust sub-paradigms: Marxism, unitarism, and pluralism. Each of them has provided explanation and insight into various aspects of LER over time. LER has been recognized for its ability to explain group-level dynamics involving employment relations.

In the dawn of this field, it covered individual-level and group-level employment relations encompassing labour laws, labour economics, personnel management and social security (Kaufman, 2008). In the decades following the 1930s, unions and collective bargaining, which is but only one component of group-level employment relations, were so successful in resolving conflicts in employment relations that the field itself became enchanted by its very success. As a result, over time, the paradigm of LER became excessively restricted to unions and collective bargaining. That academic overdependence is the problem we now face today.

Finally, practical relevance is the extent to which practical applications exists within the field (Biglan, 1973, Cox et al., 2012). Without practical relevance the field is effectively meaningless to the sustainability and advancement of society. This is especially true for applied social sciences, such as LER. The field of LER focusing on unions and collective bargaining initially had considerable practical relevance from the 1930s through the 1980s. At that time, however, the growing problem of the field was that it was becoming too dependent on union strength in, and its relevance to, society. Since the 1980s, unions have steadily declined, especially in the developed world. As a result, the field itself declined along with them, steadily losing practical relevance in the process. In turn, this loss of practical relevance has led to the closure of LER departments and the replacement of collective bargaining courses by human resource management courses, especially in US universities.

In sum, the union-focused paradigm led to the decline of practical relevance of the field. Ultimately, although ironically the subject itself seems to be growing in importance in society, its excessively narrow paradigm has reduced its practical relevance. I believe, however, as long as the subject is significant, pessimism is unwarranted. To increase the relevance of the field we must seek strategic options that can make the paradigm of LER adapt to today's social economic conditions and needs.

Three Strategies for the Revitalization of Academic Disciplines and Underlying Assumptions

Most, if not all, academic disciplines historically have faced crises of identity and foundation as human knowledge expanded or circumstances have changed. Disciplines have either ebbed (e.g. mining in some developed countries), flowed (e.g. artificial intelligence today), or even entirely disappeared (e.g. alchemy and astrology). To revitalize academic disciplines in crises, three basic strategies can be identified: strengthening the discipline itself, collaborating with other robust disciplines, and reshaping and expanding the scope of the discipline.[2] I believe these strategies are based upon distinguishable assumptions.

The first strategy suggested by Krishnan (2009) is to revitalize and reinforce the traditional boundaries separating this discipline from related disciplines. This strategy's effectiveness is predicated upon the assumption that the perceived changing environment is actually temporary and not only can but also will be reversed in due course.

Revitalization requires reemphasis of its traditional essence in terms of both theory and practice. So doing will make the discipline internally more coherent and less divisive. This strategy will enable the discipline to refocus its effort on more academically promising research (i.e. greatest return) without straying into the territory of other academic disciplines. Moreover, this strategy prevents other disciplines from intruding on its core areas. Krishnan (2009) cited the example of philosophy at the end of nineteenth century.

Jensen (2011) suggested that LER can adopt this strategy, if LER is in crisis due to temporary alteration in the political and economic environment arising from neo-liberalism that in turn has upset the balance between employer and employee in favor of the former. He opined that if this is the case, LER should not abandon its core orientation of focusing on the relationship among collective actors.

Explaining his long wave theory, Kelly (1998) observed that LER ebbs and flows cyclically in correlation with overall economic trends themselves, and thus LER scholars and practitioners should not be distracted or enticed away from the essence of LER, i.e. unions and collective bargaining, by the lure of contemporary trends. In a similar vein, Hyman (2007) asserted that the emerging model in North America and the UK will not necessarily be representative of Europe and elsewhere, where traditional LER patterns can be expected to remain resilient to contemporary threats to traditional LER structures. Thus, both asserted that continued focus on traditional LER topics such as unions and collective bargaining will prove both useful and prescient when traditional patterns reemerge and restore the luster and glory to the field of LER temporarily in crisis.

However, the obvious problem of this strategy is the extreme dependence of LER on unions and collective bargaining. As long as LER remains as a field of unions and collective bargaining, the success or failure of LER as an academic field will always be affected by the ebbs and flows of unions and collective bargaining over time, which will greatly undermine the sustainability of the academic field in attracting academic talents and maintaining academic departments.

The second strategy is to create, as Krishnan (2009) termed, "strategic alliances with stronger disciplines." To prevent obsolescence and inevitable decline into obscurity, it must collaborate with more promising, emerging, or robust disciplines. This involves removing boundaries around itself to venture forth into more academically rewarding territory by emulating and adopting relevant theories, frameworks, and approaches prevailing in other disciplines. Krishnan (2009) provided the example of the soft discipline of sociology merging with the hard discipline, biology, to form an emerging, synergistic field of "sociobiology." This strategy is premised upon two assumptions. First, it presumes that this changing landscape is not temporary but rather a permanent paradigm shift. Second, the field has little new to offer by itself as a result.

Jensen (2011) suggested that if LER utilizes this strategy, LER may incorporate itself into HRM both theoretically and methodologically. In so doing, it can shift its core to more fertile academic soil. In return, it can enable HRM to expand in a more pluralistic and less unilateral direction. This strategy, however enticing, is a double-edged sword that must be handled carefully as it poses a grave threat to the very existence of the field itself while offering the prospect of rejuvenation and resurgence through new theories and methods. The danger with this option is that the merger may result in the weaker field being entirely subsumed by the stronger, such as having future promising researchers lured by the prospect of working in a more dynamic field (Krishnan, 2009). Already we are seeing the danger beginning to materialize as some junior researchers are choosing HRM over LER. Indeed some LER departments have already adopted a hybrid LER-HRM name or even relabeled themselves as HRM.

The final strategy is readjusting, repackaging and expanding the field to incorporate emerging trends while preserving its core. This strategy may not be applicable to all fields, but only to those undergoing dynamic developments, such as experiencing new trends and paradigm shifts, that are forcing the field to expand. Newly emerging related fields offer unclaimed academic territory, creating new blue ocean strategic opportunities. This strategy is not the negation or displacement of the old; rather, increasing complexity compels the emergence of new approaches to theory, modality and methodology. For example, the discipline of Agriculture rebranded itself in the course of the last two decades as life science, thereby providing a much larger context in which to expand and thrive in multiple directions (National Research Council, 2009).

This strategy is based upon two assumptions. First, as the changing environment is irreversible, maintaining the status quo offers no prospect of restoring its old glory. This environmental irreversibility offers as much promise as threat to existing fields. Second, because of the rapidly changing environments and ever-growing complexity, there are likely to be new areas emerging that other disciplines are not likely to stake a claim over, therefore providing opportunities.

Regarding LER, there have been voices arguing for expanding the field. Such voices include Wood (2000) and Kaufman (2008). Wood (2000), in his BJIR editorial statement, proposed new directions for this discipline by arguing for broadening the scope of the field beyond unionism and collective bargaining, making the field more interdisciplinary, and further intensifying internationalization and comparative research. Kaufman (2008), comparing the original and modern paradigms of LER, lamented the narrow focus of the modern paradigm that is overly emphasizing unions and collective bargaining, and urged a return to the field's earlier, broader paradigm (i.e. original paradigm) encompassing the entirety of employment relationships in order to survive and prosper in the future.

Table 11.2 summarizes the above discussion by proposing an exploratory framework for the revitalization of academic disciplines that describes various assumptions and resulting strategies.

Table 11.2 Exploratory framework for the revitalization of academic disciplines: assumptions and resulting strategies

Strategies	Assumptions
Strategy 1: Strengthen the discipline itself.	Perceived changing environment is temporary and can be reversed.
Strategy 2: Collaborate with another robust discipline.	Changing landscape is a permanent paradigm shift. The field has little that is new to offer by itself.
Strategy 3: Reshape and expand the scope of the discipline.	Changing landscape is a permanent paradigm shift. Because of the rapidly changing environments and ever-growing complexity, there are likely to be new areas emerging.

The Case of LER: The Analyses of Strategic Options and Relevant Assumptions

As seen above, assumptions are critically important when determining which strategic option is the most pertinent. Two domains of assumptions are identified here: (1) degree of permanence of the environmental change; (2) degree of rejuvenation of the field in the face of environmental challenges. The former assumption is externally determined, whereas the latter are determined by both internal and external dynamics. The above is applied below to the field of LER to analyze its status in order to determine the proper strategy for the field.

First, when the Webbs (1902) and Commons (1918), the founders of this field, initially envisioned its scope, the field was very broad, incorporating related disciplines ranging from professional labour management (HRM), to labour law, to unions and collective bargaining, and to macroeconomic stabilization. With the rise of unions in the 1930s, following upon their growing success as an effective tool to resolve labour conflicts, unions and collective bargaining became increasingly dominant in LER to the point where in the 1960s they became the central focus of this field to the exclusion of all other sub-fields (Kaufman, 2008). This phenomenon represents a form of competency trap in which success in one sub-field eventually narrowed the entire field. Since the 1980s the socio-economic environment has changed leading to the decline of trade unionism as the dominant mechanism for labour conflict resolution, which in turn has led to deepening stagnation of the field itself.

There are reasons to believe that the decline of unions and collective bargaining is not temporary but rather represents a permanent shift in LER. Although the shift in the political landscape leading to the rise of neo-liberalism since the early 1980s has certainly accelerated the stagnation of trade unionism, two fundamental trends in employment relations are currently driving the stagnation of unions and collective bargaining. On one hand, we are witnessing the transformation of societal dynamics from bilateral (i.e. conflicts between capital vs. labour) to multilateral (i.e. conflicts surrounding the issue of identity groups such as women, minorities, immigrants) since the human rights movement arising from the 1960s (Piore and Safford, 2006). Trade unions, however, are still largely based upon the capital-labour dichotomy emphasized in earlier eras. Labour unions are still often based on the idea that it is best to unite all types of labour together to confront capital, but this might not be realistic in today's society. Thus, there will be limits imposed on the growth of unions in the future society increasingly characterized by multilateral structures. Indeed. identity-based labour organizations such as quasi-unions, labour centers, and civil society organizations are increasingly emerging outside traditional unions, as shown through growing attention among researchers and practitioners (Heckscher and Carre, 2006; Heery, Abbott and Williams, 2012).

On the other hand, the Fourth Industrial Revolution poses another threat to trade unionism. The increasing number of freelance and on-demand workers (e.g. Uber drivers) in the gig economy spurred by the Fourth Industrial Revolution is resulting in weaker attachment of the present workforce to enterprises, as shown by the increasing number of dependent self-employed workers. In essence, current employment seems to be returning to the free labour market of the nineteenth century, which is often referred to as "labour nomad" (Weil, 2014). Since unions have traditionally thrived on stable employment relations, the general trend of weakening attachment of workers to enterprises is inevitably leading to the decline of trade unionism. In the past, union vitality cyclically ebbed and flowed like the tide (Kelly, 1998); however, there is a growing consensus that we are now witnessing a permanent paradigm shift in labour relations (Weil, 2014). Therefore, there is emerging pessimism that unions will not resurge to their former glory, although unions, in the form of so-called ghetto-unionism, can be expected to remain entrenched in some sectors such as large-scale manufacturing and public sectors. The general societal and technological transformations are progressing slowly but steadily and seem to be irreversible.

The implication is that consequently a substantial minority, at a minimum, of workers in the future will not be able to or simply will not choose unions and collective bargaining as their main advocate and weapon. Instead, they will increasingly turn to new actors, such as civil society organizations, employment rights organizations, labour NGOs (non-governmental organizations), quasi-unions, internet-based voice channels and various non-union voice channels to promote their interests. This chapter does not argue that unions and collective bargaining will entirely disappear in the future. A more realistic projection is that unions will still remain as one of the main modes regulating employment relations; however, future employment relations are expected to be much more diverse.

Second, this field has room for expansion in terms of actors, issues and approaches to conflict resolution, given the growing complexity of the area of employment relations arising from the current changing environment. Almost daily we observe in headlines diverse labour issues arising. Labour problems are becoming increasingly severe and important due to economic polarization and rapid technical advances; yet, ironically, our field is in crisis. That is because despite the growing societal attention to labour issues, this field fails to address the problem "in a way that has captured the public's imagination" (Delaney, 2006: 500). As a result, the general public does not fully appreciate this academic field as important. Judging from today's headlines dealing with labour problems, the issues involving labour as a whole are expanding beyond the traditional boundaries of LER that is largely limited to unions and collective bargaining. This field has to be readjusted and reconstructed in order to meet the changing social needs that are increasingly beyond the existing paradigm of unions and collective bargaining.

Clearly, an expanded focus is called for. We have to guide LER to expand beyond a rigid focus on unions and collective bargaining.

First, this field must embrace rising new actors in the area of employment relations such as quasi-unions, labour NGOs, and civil society organizations. These organizations typically encompass, among others, various identity groups such as women, minorities, elderly, and physically challenged workers, all of whom traditional unions have tended to overlook. That is, this field should expand from its focus on capital-labour dichotomy to incorporate the multi-dimensional socio-economic relations among various identity groups. In doing so, we can attempt more alignment with sociology and its student of social movements and worker protest, and political science with its study of political actors.

We are observing a decline in the number of strikes in most developed countries; however, this is not due to increased labour tranquility (Gall and Hebdon, 2008). Rather, the form of labour disputes are mutating into new forms including demonstrations and protests that increasingly utilize social media because many workers cannot conduct strikes due to the inability to join unions. Even those who can often lack sufficient bargaining power to conduct effective strikes. This field must embrace new forms of labour disputes in addition to strikes.

Traditionally, this field primarily concentrated on the labour issues of developed industrial countries, and accordingly put less importance on labour problems in developing countries. Now, however, the importance of developing countries in the political and economic sense is steadily increasing. Therefore, we have to pay more attention to them. The conventional theoretical framework formulated from the experiences of developed countries does not adequately explain LER in emerging economies. For example, unions in developing countries create unique patterns of unionism distinctive from the Euro-American pattern (Ng, Lansbury and Lee, 2019). Also, the role of the state in labour relations is a highly critical factor in all aspects of labour relations in developing countries. Yet, the pluralistic tradition of LER denies such role in its theoretical framework (Hyman, 2008). Consequently, Western textbooks that students in developing countries are currently using at schools are not well adapted to many LER phenomena around world. To attract ever increasing students and practitioners from emerging economies, the field must be made relevant to their world. Clearly, a new theoretical framework that acknowledges the deterministic role of the state in developing countries is urgently required.

LER has a long tradition of studying the relationship between technology and labour (Braverman, 1974; Marx, 1967; Piore and Sabel, 1986). Given the nature of the Fourth Industrial Revolution currently underway, this relationship is expected to greatly intensify. Thus, this field must claim ownership of this domain within its academic scope. Otherwise, the related academic fields of technology (such as artificial intelligence) and labour can and will be claimed by neighboring fields. LER must expand to embrace technical revolution and human labour. Possible, indeed even likely, research topics include: under which conditions can technology help workers perform their jobs more efficiently and effectively; whether technology dominates humans through oversight and even direction in workplaces; under which conditions can technology entirely replace human labour; how the dramatic introduction of technology (e.g. artificial intelligence, bionics, implantation of devices into human bodies; physical fusion between humans and technology) in workplaces alter existing LER.

Moreover, employment relations are changing under the gig economy characterized by weaker worker attachment to the firm. This development is greatly undermining a critical theoretical assumption of traditional LER, the existence of stable employment relations between workers and firms. Under the gig economy, unions and collective bargaining themselves are likely to assume very different forms. Needless to say, we need to develop a new theoretical framework to encompass this emerging phenomenon accelerated by the Fourth Industrial Revolution.

Another obvious issue is the growing incompatibility between existing labour law and the evolving world of work outlined above. Fundamentally revising labour laws to align with existing and future reality will be an urgent task. Accordingly, we also can incorporate the legal labour domain within LER. In brief, the above offers a few examples of the many emerging domains that LER could subsume in due course.

In sum, considering the revitalization of academic disciplines, three strategies and their assumptions were presented (See Table 11.2). The above discussion suggests that the third strategy is most appropriate for LER, because the field is experiencing a permanent paradigm shift; and there are likely to be new areas emerging due to the rapidly changing environments and their dynamic interactions characterized by ever-growing complexity.

Conclusion: Do We Really Want to Be Twenty-first Century Luddites?

Over the years, various academic organizations in our field have changed their names to reflect the concerns expressed above (i.e. excessively narrow focus on unions and collective bargaining to the detriment of emerging employment structures). For example, in the last decade, the International Industrial Relations Association (IIRA), Industrial Relations Research Association (IRRA), and Korea Industrial

Relations Association (KIRA) changed their names to International Labour and Employment Relations (ILERA), Labour and Employment Relations Association (LERA), and Korea Labour and Employment Relations Association (KLERA), respectively.

Despite the initiatives of such academic associations, our results suggest that LER is still a field of unions and collective bargaining. Our field must embrace the new world of work. Failing to do so will make our field increasingly irrelevant to the growing number of non-traditional actors. Accordingly, to remain relevant to the fast-changing global world of work, we need to expand the paradigm of this field by conducting more active research on the following: artificial intelligence and employment relations in the Fourth Industrial Revolution era; emerging alternative representative bodies (such as civil society organizations, employment rights organizations, labour NGOs, and quasi-unions); new forms of labour disputes; employment relations of freelance and on-demand workers in the gig economy; LER in developing countries; and labour law compatible with the requisites of the new world of work; all of which are growing in importance as they advance from the periphery to the center of labour relations and practices globally.

However, I am not suggesting outright abandonment of unions and collective bargaining. I believe that we must also preserve our traditional core in addition to the above. Unions and collective bargaining may decline but are likely to remain one of the critical components of LER in the future society. Most likely, unions and collective bargaining will maintain their importance in large manufacturing companies and the public sector, where unions remain deeply entrenched. Unions and collective bargaining may be stagnant now in developed countries, but can rebound in different forms in the future. That said, however, unions and collective bargaining is not now and certainly will not be the only form going forward.

In conclusion, it is obvious that LER has been trapped by its own past success. However, opportunity often comes in the guise of crisis. As long as the subject of this field, labour problems, remains essential to modern society, we need not be discouraged. Now is time for a bold strategic decision for the revitalization of LER. If we do not want to be twenty-first century Luddites, we have to readjust, reconfigure and expand the field to incorporate emerging trends while preserving its core.

Acknowledgments

I acknowledge the research assistance of Ki Jung Kim, Peter Sylvestre, Kyung Yoen Kim, and Minju Shin, and thank Paula Voos and Russell Lansbury for their helpful comments.

Notes

1 The reason union studies maintain their prominence in these LER journals could be that it has become harder over time to publish studies about unions elsewhere as their perceived relevance declined. Top journals in neighboring fields such as management, economics, and sociology might have been more likely to publish an article on unions in earlier years than now.

2 Krishnan (2009) provided four strategies: reinforcement of traditional boundaries; subordination to a stronger discipline; embedding within a stronger field with the objective of eventual domination; union with other endangered disciplines to form a new field. Among them the first two are applicable to LER and similar to the first two strategies developed in this chapter.

References

Biglan, A. (1973) "The Characteristics of Subject Matter in Different Academic Areas," *Journal of Applied Psychology*, 57(3), pp. 195-203.

Braverman, H. (1974) *Labour and Monopoly Capital*, Monthly Review.

Budd, J. (2004) *Employment with a Human Face: Balancing Efficiency, Equity and Voice*, ILR Press.

Commons, J.R. (1918) *History of Labour in the United States*, Macmillan.

Cox, M.Z., Daspit, J., Mclaughlin, E. and Jones III, R.J. (2012) "Strategic Management: Is it an Academic Discipline?," *Journal of Business Strategies*, 29(1), pp. 25-42.

Delaney, J.T. (2006) "The Flattening of Industrial Relations," *Review Symposium: Global Evolution of Industrial Relations. Industrial and Labour Relations Review*, 59(3), pp. 497-501.

Gall, G. and Hebdon, R. (2008) "Conflict at Work," in Blyton, P., Bacon, N., Fiorito, J. and Heery, E. (eds.), *The SAGE Handbook of Industrial Relations*, SAGE Publication, pp. 588-605.

Heckscher, C., and Carre, F. (2006) "Strength in Networks: Employment Rights Organizations and the Problem of Co-ordination," *British Journal of Industrial Relations*, 44(4), pp. 605-628.

Heery, E., Abbott, B., and Williams, S. (2012) "The Involvement of Civil Society Organizations in British Industrial Relations: Extent, Origins and Significance," *British Journal of Industrial Relations*, 50(1), pp. 47-72.

Hyman, R. (2007) "An Anglo-European Perspective on Industrial Relations Research," *Arbetsmarknad & Arbetsliv*, 13(3-4), pp. 29-41.

Hyman, R. (2008) "The State in Industrial Relations," in Blyton, P., Bacon, N., Fiorito, J. and Heery, E. (eds.), *The Sage Handbook of Industrial Relations*, Sage Publication, pp. 258-283.

Jensen, C.S. (2011) "Between Industrial and Employment Relations - the Practical and Academic Implications of Changing Labour Markets," *Arbetsmarknad & Arbetsliv*, 17(3).

Kaufman, B.E. (2008) "Paradigms in Industrial Relations: Original, Modern and Versions In-between," *British Journal of Industrial Relations*, 46(2), pp. 314-339.

Kelly, J. (1998) *Rethinking Industrial Relations - Mobilisations, Collectivism and Long Waves*, Routledge.

Kim, D.-O. and Kim. K.J. (2018) *Trend Analyses of Employment Relations Studies 1947-2014: Implication for Future Research Strategy*. A Paper Presented at the 18th International Labour and Employment Relations Association (ILERA), 2018 World Congress, Seoul, Korea.

Kochan, T.A. (1998) "What is Distinctive about Industrial Relations Research?," In Whitfield, K. and Strauss, G. (eds.), *Researching the World of Work*, ILR Press, pp 31-50.

Krishnan, A. (2009) *What Are Academic Disciplines? Some Observations on the Disciplinarity vs. Interdisciplinarity Debate*. Working Paper, University of Southhampton National Centre for Research Methods.

Kuhn, T.S. (1996) *The Structure of Scientific Revolutions* (3rd edn.), University of Chicago Press.

Marx, K. (1967) *Capital: A Critique of Political Economy*, International Publishers.

McDivitt, J. (2002) *Status of Education of Mining Industry Professionals*. International Institute for Environment and Development (Mining, Minerals and Sustainable Development), No.3. London, United Kingdom: International Institute for Environment and Development.

National Research Council. (2009) *Transforming Agricultural*

Education for a Changing World, National Academic Press.

Ng, S., Lansbury, R. D. and Lee, B.-H. (2019, forthcoming) "Perspectives on Asian Unionism as a Regional Pattern," in Lee, B.-H., Ng, S., Russell, D.L. (eds.), *Trade Unions and Labour Movements in the Asia-Pacific Region*, Routledge.

Piore, M.J. and Sable, C.F. (1986) *The Second Industrial Divide: Possibilities for Prosperity*, Basic Books.

Piore, M.J. and Safford, S. (2006) "Changing Regimes of Workplace Governance, Shifting Axes of Social Mobilization, and the Challenge to Industrial Relations Theory," *Industrial Relations*, 45(3), pp. 299-325.

Visser, J. (2006) "Union Membership Statistics in 24 Countries," *Monthly Labour Review*, 129, pp. 38-49.

Webb, S. and Webb, B. (1902) *Industrial Democracy*, Longman.

Weil, D. (2014) T*he Fissured Workplace: Why Work Became So Bad for So Many and What Can Be Done to Improve It*, Harvard University Press.

Wood, S. (2000) "The British Journal of Industrial Relations and Industrial Relations in the New Millennium," *British Journal of Industrial Relations*, 38(1), pp. 1-5.

NAME INDEX

T

V

W

SUBJECT INDEX

D

H

I

N

O

P

Q

R

S

Y